The Hurricane Book

Advance Praise for *The Hurricane Book*

"In *The Hurricane Book,* Claudia Acevedo-Quiñones draws an unflinching ecology of intimacy, a swirling account of that mythical pair of words we all fear and love: family and country. History has rarely felt so vivid, so candid, so potent."

—Carlos Fonseca, author of *Austral*

"*The Hurricane Book* is an important work of art and archive, a blend of poetry, cartography, and Puerto Rican history. Alternating between playful language and sobering reality, Claudia Acevedo-Quiñones interrogates memory and truth, explores family secrets, and sheds light on the realities of colonialism. A multilayered, powerful book—*The Hurricane Book* is a gift."

—Jaquira Díaz, author of *Ordinary Girls: A Memoir*

The Hurricane Book

a lyric history

Claudia Acevedo-Quiñones

Rose Metal Press

2023

Rose Metal Press, Inc.
P.O. Box 1956, Brookline, MA 02446
rosemetalpress@gmail.com
www.rosemetalpress.com

Some names and identifying details such as physical properties, occupations, and places of residence have been changed to protect the privacy of individuals. I have tried to recreate events, locales, and conversations from my memories of them.

Library of Congress Cataloging-in-Publication Data

Names: Acevedo-Quiñones, Claudia, 1988- author.
Title: The hurricane book : a lyric history / by Claudia Acevedo-Quiñones.
Description: Brookline, MA : Rose Metal Press, 2023.
Identifiers: LCCN 2023031011 (print) | LCCN 2023031012 (ebook) | ISBN
   9781941628317 (print) | ISBN 9781941628324 (e-book)
Subjects: LCSH: Acevedo-Quiñones, Claudia, 1988- | Acevedo-Quiñones,
   Claudia, 1988---Family. | Puerto Ricans--New York (State)--New
   York--Biography. | Puerto Ricans--Biography. | Puerto Rico--Biography. |
   Puerto Rico--Social conditions. | Hurricanes--Puerto Rico. | New York
   (N.Y.)--Biography.
Classification: LCC F128.9.P85 A34 2023 (print) | LCC F128.9.P85 (ebook)
   | DDC 972.95092 [B]--dc23/eng/20230705
LC record available at https://lccn.loc.gov/2023031011
LC ebook record available at https://lccn.loc.gov/2023031012

Cover artwork and design by Jason Alejandro
Interior design by Heather Butterfield

The text on the cover is set in Libre Baskerville, a humanist serif font designed by Pablo Impallari in 2011. It's based on a version of Baskerville that was released by American Type Founders in 1941, but the first Baskerville face was designed by John Baskerville in 1757. The interior text is set in traditional Baskerville, with Cabinet Grotesk used for headings and Romana used for the decorative section breaks.

This book is manufactured in the United States of America and printed on acid-free paper.

Para Julia, Jesús y Lourdes. Con las tripas en la mano.

"[…] Llevaré siempre la mancha/ por secula seculorum."

"[…] I'll always carry the stain/ for ever and ever."

—from "La mancha de plátano" by Luis Lloréns Torres (1876–1944)

Author's Note

While much of *The Hurricane Book* is autobiographical, I can't and don't claim to fully know what is true or false about real people's private histories, thoughts, or intentions—much less those of people I've only ever heard about or imagined. (I also imagine and misremember people I know!)

For this reason, I have changed people's names and sometimes other identifying characteristics throughout the book. There are also degrees of speculation and fictionalization where certain events I had no part in are concerned. Throughout the book, I point out where something may not have actually happened, or may not have happened in the way described, or could be considered fiction, depending on whom you ask.

The above does not apply to the "Historical Notes," or to the hurricane essays directly following those, which deal with hurricane-related statistics. Nor does it apply to anything occurring solely to me. Yet even then, there is always room for error. I have a difficult time trusting myself, which is part of the reason why I write.

This lack of trust led me to experiment with hybrid forms in recent years. I need to consider all potential outcomes and employ every approach and perspective at my disposal before I feel confident enough to make a statement. Before I was able to let go of my adherence to "form" and "genre," poetry was my preferred outlet. I could make the storytelling process (and myself) as messy or neat, as concrete or abstract, as I wanted. Prose in the regular sense—clean transitions, continuity, plot—didn't come easily to me. I dealt in stilted lines, fragmented images, and incomplete thoughts. I abandoned the first draft of this book 14 years ago, during my third year in the United States, because I didn't think I could lean into that way of writing a story.

At that time, I wanted this book to be a chronological account of my maternal family's move from Galicia, Spain to Puerto Rico in the 1600s. I stopped writing it after 40 pages. I stopped writing regularly for years. When I did write, I opted for flash fiction and poems that told stories I felt I had the right to tell: mainly from my own romantic life, or the stories of people and inanimate objects who couldn't talk back.

In 2017, I recommitted to writing seriously. I quit my job in publishing and enrolled in an MFA program. There, I attended workshops in all genres, but joined as a poet. My goal was to leave Stony Brook University with 20 to 30 poems I could turn into a publishable collection.

Then, during my first month of grad school, Hurricane María hit Puerto Rico. Even though I'd left the island more than a decade prior, I hadn't felt the weight of my choice to leave quite as soberly as when the island was going through that particular catastrophe, one of many happening concurrently. I decided to go back to the original draft of this book, to the story of the ancestors who, like me, had left their place of birth.

Estrangement and distance warp memory. They influence one's treatment of a place. There was no way I could've gone back to the draft without acknowledging that I was a white member of the Puerto Rican diaspora who had been assimilating and in the land of the colonizer for 17 years, and that I was trying to piece together a multi-pronged story with many missing pieces. I realized that I couldn't write the story in a strictly narrative way and started to conceptualize a hybrid way to tell it.

I began by writing down what I knew for sure, what was at the forefront. Like any Puerto Rican, I am intimately familiar with hurricanes. We know when and how to put up a storm window, what we need to keep in our pantry, how to pass the time when there's no power. While reconstructing and deconstructing Puerto Rican historico-politics and my family's history—a process that is flawed and objectively ever-changing—I structured my work around something that I could directly speak to and that has, without question, influenced how we live and what we endure and recover from. As the book took shape, I built it around six major hurricanes, beginning each section with historical facts about that era in Puerto Rico and factual details about the hurricane. I then tied my family and personal history to the same eras and hurricanes.

I grounded what I knew about hurricanes in research. Archival photography, weather maps, old newspaper clippings, databases, and U.S. census documents were essential to the process. Those same census documents led me to ancestry websites, which, while occasionally inaccurate or incomplete, produced birth and marriage certificates, draft cards, and surprising information about people I had only heard about in drunken spill sessions. I went on statistical tangents, talked to meteorologists, transcribed poems by family members, and translated half-remembered conversations. I started to be able to make connections between historical and private events, facts and hearsay, things that were kept quiet and painful lived experience. I would love to say that this project gave me absolute clarity, or some sort of justification for my and my family's decisions to leave Puerto Rico or stay, but this wasn't the case. I *can* say that my confusion about what we've done and what has been done to us, while not gone, has become more layered, textured, and open to other sources of confusion.

The only way I can feel like I've told a "true" story responsibly is by making it as much about the process as it is about what is being told. My process is imperfect, scattered, and not the most efficient. But I hope it's fair. Writing a memoir is not necessarily cathartic. It's more like dredging sediment. Coming to terms with both my personal history and the realities of Puerto Rico's past and present stirred up a lot for me.

But ultimately, I didn't only write this book for me. It felt essential to tell my story in a way that also illuminated Puerto Rico's long and deep-seated relationship with the uncertainty and trauma brought on by colonialism, in addition to its beauty. I wanted to show how the impact of that history, intensified by weather, is felt by the island's ecosystems, residents, and diaspora, and seeps into our families and lives. I hope the book will resonate and reveal, appealing to the scattered and murky parts of us that want to feel less messed up and alone.

Contents

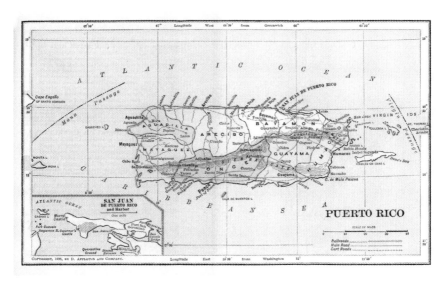

Map of Puerto Rico from 1898 including Mona (on the southwest), Vieques, and Culebra (east of the big island).

House Key

Yaya, The Extreme Vital Principle,
Killed His Own Son, Yayael,
For Fear Of Losing His Kingdom.

He Kept His Son's Remains In A Güiro Basket,
Which Hung From The Ceiling Of His Bohío,
A Basket Stolen By Deminán Caracaracol,
Who Knew The Secret To Making Cassava,
Secrets He Learned From Bayamonaco, Spirit Of Fire,
Who Upon Hearing About The Theft,
Spit On Caracaracol,
Which Produced Caguama, The Turtle.

Caguama, Mother Of Arawaks,
Turtle Mother,
Whose Meat Fed This Side Of The Antilles,
Whose Orphaned Children Cried Along The River Banks,
And Made Co-quís Spring From Hungry Frogs.

Then Yúcahu Bagua Maorocote/Yocahú/Yukiyú, God Of Cassava And
    The Sea,
He Who Has No Father,
He Who Has No Desire,
He Who Watches Over Men And Women,
He Who Has No Other Purpose,
Whose Mother Atabey, Goddess Of The Moon And Fecundity,

Oversees The Flowering Of The Earth And The Harvest With Him,
He Whose Likeness In Stone Nurtures The Seed.

Then Guabancex, Woman Storm, Goddess Of Winds And Hurricanes,
Who With Her Two Assistants,
Guatauba, Gatherer Of Rains And Lightning,
And Cotrisquie, Gatherer Of Waters,
Destroys Conucos When The People In Them Have Not Rendered
The Tribute Due To Her Image.

Borikén, Land Of Noble Lords,
Is Prone To Disasters.

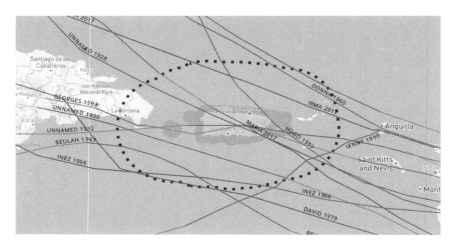

Trajectory of major land-falling cyclones (categories 3, 4, and 5) in Puerto Rico from 1928 to 2017.

I. Hurricane San Felipe II

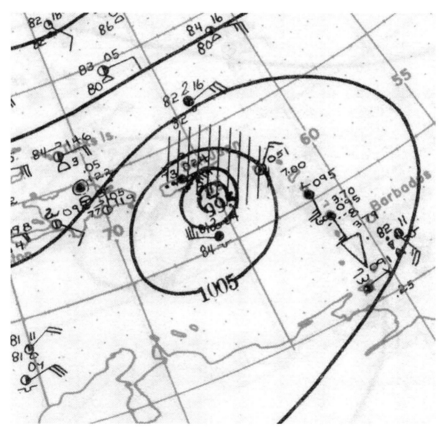

Weather map of San Felipe Segundo nearing Puerto Rico on September 13, 1928.

Maternal Family Tree

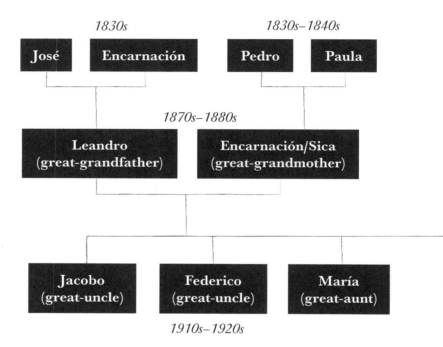

1830s   *1830s–1840s*

| José | Encarnación | | Pedro | Paula |

1870s–1880s

| Leandro (great-grandfather) | Encarnación/Sica (great-grandmother) |

| Jacobo (great-uncle) | Federico (great-uncle) | María (great-aunt) |

1910s–1920s

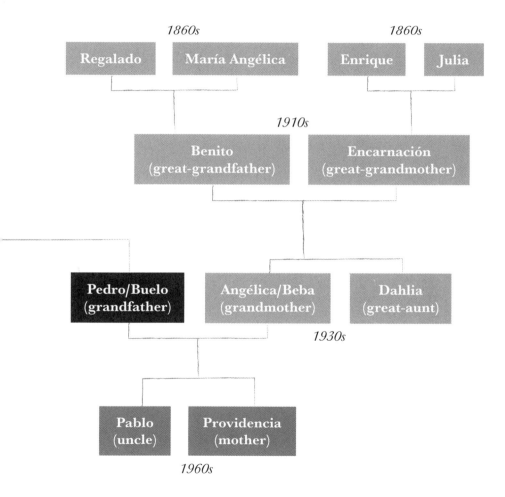

Historical Notes

Puerto Rico is made of volcanic rock. It is located between the Atlantic Ocean and the Caribbean Sea, on the boundary of the Caribbean and North American plates, and at one of the three points of the Devil's Triangle, also known as the Bermuda Triangle, a setting for inexplicable shipwrecks and airplane crashes.

≈

Borikén is Puerto Rico's Arawak name, used by the Taíno people who settled on the island between the 7th and 11th centuries.

≈

Before Western science confirmed it, the Taínos knew that hurricanes had eyes. Their cemíes, or ceramic icons, featured faces with arms spiraling in opposite directions.

≈

They planted yuca and yautía. Root crops could resist strong winds.

≈

The Caribs of the Lesser Antilles factored in hurricane season, the worst of which is over by October, when planning their raids of Borikén. When Ursa Minor, "the canoe of the heron," appeared in the night sky after the summer solstice, this was their signal to begin preparing for war, which usually happened between late September and December.

≈

Bartolomé de las Casas was a 16th-century Spanish priest who witnessed the first wave of genocides in the New [Old] World. In 1542, he wrote *A Brief*

Account of the Destruction of the Indies, in which he deemed the Caribbean Islands "pitiful," their inhabitants "humble," "clean," and "docile." In a moment of poetic empathy, he likened the Spanish conquerors' behavior to that of "ravening wild beasts, wolves, tigers, or lions that had been starved for many days." This was meant to convince Prince Philip II of Spain to put a stop to the carnage perpetrated by their countrymen, who, after arriving in 1492, defiled San Juan (one of Puerto Rico's early names) and more than 30 other islands. De las Casas estimated that by the 1520s, 2,100 leagues of land were uninhabited.

≈

In the name of Catholicism, the Spanish pillaged native lands and raped their people. They stabbed, dismembered, and cut Taínos to pieces "as if dealing with sheep in the slaughterhouse." They made bets to see who could split a man in two with the stroke of a pike. They took infants from their mothers and threw them in the rivers. In the memory of their Redeemer and his 12 apostles, they hanged their victims in gallows and burned them alive.

≈

To restore the island's population, de las Casas suggested importing slaves from Africa, a decision he later regretted.

≈

Puerto Rico went on to become an important port for the Spanish Empire, but remained scarcely populated due to the lure of the more prosperous territories in South America.

≈

In the 1800s, when the rest of the Americas were freeing themselves from Spain, Puerto Rico and Cuba remained colonized. In 1897, the liberal Spanish government agreed to the Charters of Autonomy of Cuba and

Puerto Rico, which allowed the islands to govern themselves as overseas provinces of the Empire.

≈

On July 25, 1898, U.S. soldiers led by General Nelson Appleton Miles invaded Puerto Rico through the Guánica Bay.

≈

We have been U.S. citizens without voting representatives since 1917.

Pedro/Buelo

Hurricane San Felipe II
Caguas
September 13, 1928

When you are born a jíbaro
into a heap of tobacco leaves
three months after the wind
takes down the family farmhouse
you look for a roof at the bottom of a glass
for the rest of your life.
You walk to school with no shoes on
and a cigarette in your mouth.
You don't pray; you raise yourself better
than your parents did.
And because the worst has already happened
at a hundred miles an hour,
you look people in the eye
and tell them the truth.
You enlist in a stranger's army
to help feed your brothers,
and play the same game of war for a decade
and never complain.
You plant aloe and grapefruit and mango
to feed your wife
with the same macheted hand
you were dealt.

You punch in and out in the same brown suit
every day
to feed your daughter
before cocktail hour,
before feeding yourself.
You kill a rabid dog
with a can of sardines
to stay alive
for your daughter's daughter,
who looks to the bottom of your glass
for a roof.

Hurricane San Felipe II

San Felipe II was the most powerful hurricane to strike Puerto Rico up to that point. It was called San Felipe because it passed through the island on September 13, the feast of Saint Philip; not Philip the apostle, but Philip the martyr, father of Saint Eugenia and husband to Claudia. He and his wife renounced their political life in Alexandria and converted to Christianity. This was after Eugenia ran away from home to live as a man in a monastery and was wrongfully accused of seduction by a besotted woman she had healed. Eugenia bared her breasts to a confused Philip, who happened to be the prefect overseeing her trial, in an attempt to prove her innocence. Because a woman could never seduce another woman. It was called San Felipe *II* because it was the second time a hurricane blew through the island on that same day in September.

≈

When it hit the Caribbean, on September 12, San Felipe II was already a Category 3, and only strengthened after crossing Guadeloupe that day. When it made landfall in southeastern Puerto Rico, it was as a Category 5 storm, carrying winds of up to 160 mph. The mountains in the Cordillera Central got up to 30 inches of rain. The death toll was over 300. Over 20,000 homes were completely destroyed, and almost 200,000 suffered damages. Tobacco, citrus, coffee, and sugar crops were destroyed. It is estimated that the hurricane cost the island $50 million in crop and property losses. This is in 1928 USD, roughly $855 million in 2022.

≈

Nearly 1,500 people died in the Caribbean alone. Most buildings in Guadeloupe were flattened. Farmers in Montserrat nearly starved before relief got to them.

≈

When San Felipe II made landfall in West Palm Beach, Florida, it was a Category 4 hurricane with winds of up to 150 mph. It caused a 10-ft storm surge. Before weakening along the coasts of eastern Georgia and the Carolinas, it crossed Lake Okeechobee. While the exact death toll wasn't confirmed, between 1,770 and 2,500 people died there, which is why San Felipe II is mostly known as the Okeechobee hurricane.

≈

"Yuquiyú está furioso. ¿Te fijas como de pronto hinchó la corriente?"

"Yuquiyú is angry. See how all of a sudden he swelled up the current?"

> —Marcela in *La Víspera del Hombre* (1958) by
> René Marqués (1919–1979), which is set in Puerto Rico
> and begins in the months leading up to San Felipe II.

Sica

Sica, my mother's paternal grandmother, came from a long line of farmers who had never left the Caguas Valley.

≈

She woke up at 5:00 a.m. every day. She washed her face, braided her hair, and went to the kitchen to prepare breakfast. Hard bread, a couple of melon wedges, and goat's milk. No one in the house ever complained, even though they knew that their lunch and dinner would look exactly like breakfast.

≈

She took pleasure in small things. She was proud of her long, black hair. She enjoyed smoking cigars she rolled herself. She drank cognac, which she kept in the trunk by her bed.

≈

My grandfather, his brothers, and sister went through life free to roam, smoke, and drink whatever they wanted. By the time he was 11, my grandfather, Pedro, carried cigarettes in his pockets. By the time he was 15, he had a tolerance for rum.

≈

Leandro was Pedro's father. For most of his adult life, Leandro was in jail for homicide. A neighbor had propositioned his oldest son, my grandfather's big brother Jacobo, so he killed him with a machete.

≈

My grandfather was the first person in his family to attend university.

≈

On his way to school one day, a pit bull attacked my grandfather. The dog bit off a chunk of his leg. He whipped out the can of sardines he had in his lunchbox and beat him on the head with it until the dog was dead or close to it. He disinfected the wound on his leg with urine. The scar was barely visible, from what I can remember.

≈

My mother says Sica was the softest, gentlest person alive. She had gone through so much loss, letting things slide was probably the best approach to dealing with children and bad times. After her husband was imprisoned, Jacobo worked in the United States so he could help support his mother and send my grandfather, his youngest brother, to university. My grandfather, who considered Jacobo a father figure, said he worked in a quarry. My mother said he worked on farms. Either way, Jacobo came back to Caguas after he was able to save up a little bit of money. He and Sica shared a home, which my grandfather Pedro visited with my mother and uncle every Sunday. They'd bring her peach concentrate and tobacco.

≈

My grandfather's enabling of their mother's smoking seemed to be the only point of contention between Jacobo and him. In 1978, Sica died at 97 in her kitchen. She collapsed by the stove. Jacobo, who never married, died the same year I was born, 10 years after his mother.

Plantation and sugar mill in Caguas circa 1900.

Old Wives' Tales

My mother's mother said to not let anyone sweep over my feet unless I wanted to end up a jamona[1], an old maid and a waste of good woman.

A broom poked out my great-aunt María's eye while she swept. My grandmother told me not to worry, because she had a third one. And it could see the ghosts of our loved ones, and the most prominent features of people we hadn't met yet. After cataracts blinded her second eye, María didn't stop holding séances. I'd sit in the living room and stare at the horseshoes nailed to the walls and the crosses stitched to the cushions, and measure the distance between me and any brooms, and pray with my eyes open for my grandmother and her sister-in-law to be done summoning spirits in the kitchen.

María's son did his best to hide her saint candles after she went blind. But she kept finding and lighting them until her house burned down.

So I am careful when I sweep.

---

[1] The literal translation of "jamona" is "female ham." According to *Urban Dictionary*, jamonas are "women notorious for their sad lonely eyes and their irrational love for their pets."

Rock River

The Otero-Gaviños, my mother's mother's grandparents, immigrated to Puerto Rico from Galicia, northern Spain, in the 1910s. The name Otero comes from the Galician outeiro, meaning "knoll," an isolated hill. The name Galicia is derived from the Latin Gallaecia, home of the Celtic Gallaeci tribe, who helped Lusitania fight against the Romans in the mid-2nd century BC. The roots gall- and kall- suggest "stone" or "rock" in Celtic and Proto-Celtic, respectively. Folk etymology suggests that Gallaeci comes from the Greek word for milk, gála, which was used to describe the fair skin of the Galicians. Galicia is wild, mountainous, full of hard edges and dips. It is known as "o país dos mil ríos." The country of a thousand rivers.

≈

My grandmother Angélica spoke of her own grandmother's hard temperament, her fits of anger and coolness toward her children. When she was angry, she would say, *Mira, que se me sale lo gallego. Watch out, the Galician's spilling out.* She died of anemia. *You're hard as rock*, my father used to tell me.

≈

My grandmother's mother met her husband at the Plaza de Armas, one of the main squares in Old San Juan, when they were both in their early twenties. They married and had two daughters, Angélica and Dahlia. There are Plazas de Armas in Cajamarca, Lima, Havana, Santiago, Manila, Antigua, Guadalajara, San Antonio, and other cities built by Spanish colonizers. "Arma" means "weapon." If you replace the "r" with an "l," you get the word for "soul." The squares were commonly placed in a convenient, central location from which arms could be distributed in the event of an attack.

≈

After her husband died during delirium tremens, my great-grandmother moved the family to Loíza, in the northeast, west of the Río Grande (Big River), and found work as a seamstress, which left my grandmother in charge of the household. My great-aunt Dahlia was her father's favorite when he was alive. She was twice crowned Queen of the Loíza Carnival and got paid to wave to people from a float stark naked save for some strategically placed tulle and seashells. She married an older man she met at a club and became a travel agent. My great-grandmother found a second husband, a sweet man who worked at an airport, and had a third daughter, Sandra, who loved The Monkees and married a guy she met at a stoplight.

≈

After high school, Angélica headed to the town of Río Piedras (Rock River), where a friend offered her a job as a teller in the Banco Popular. She had been in love with Braulio Castillo, a classmate who went on to star in popular telenovelas and movies, but they fell out of touch soon after graduation. He quit acting after he was hit on the head by a big rock during the filming of *Heaven and You* in 1970. In it, he played a Catholic priest with amnesia who ends up falling in love with Irán Eory in a hippie commune. He died in 2015, three years after my grandmother.

" […]
Río Grande de Loíza!... Blue. Brown. Red.
Blue mirror, fallen piece of blue sky;
naked white flesh that turns black
each time the night enters your bed;
red stripe of blood, when the rain falls
in torrents and the hills vomit their mud.

Man river, but man with the purity of river,
because you give your blue soul when you give your blue kiss.

Most sovereign river mine. Man river. The only man
who has kissed my soul upon kissing my body.

Río Grande de Loíza!... Great river. Great flood of tears.
The greatest of all our island's tears
save those greater that come from the eyes
of my soul for my enslaved people."

—from "Río Grande de Loíza" by Julia de Burgos
(1914–1953), translated by Jack Agüeros

Oldsmobile

Buelo (my name for abuelo Pedro) drove a blue 1984 Oldsmobile Cutlass Ciera with a baby blue velvet interior. It smelled like cigarettes, Agua Maravilla, and pomade. He'd ride in it with the windows down and the radio on, leaning back on the seat as far as possible, with one liverspotted hand on the wheel and the other holding a lit Marlboro Red. Sometimes there would be a Coors Light in the cupholder. Coors Light is basically water. The easiest parent to spot at school pickup was my grandfather. He'd always be there waiting, or just pulling up to put out his cigarette on the sidewalk, at 2:10 p.m. sharp. If for any reason he couldn't make it on time, he'd call the principal's assistant and ask her to tell me his ETA over the classroom intercom. For 10 years, I could count on him being there to pick me up. Thin, wiry, pockmarked, annoyed, impeccably dressed, uninterested in socializing with the rich mothers he barely tolerated. There were Range Rovers and Hummers everywhere then. My classmates wore Tiffany charm bracelets. That was Guaynabo in the 2000s. Buelo was a relic. I liked to pretend he was my chauffeur father, like in *Sabrina*. He'd load up my rolling backpack and ask about my day. I liked watching the dust and smoke poof up from the velvet whenever I punched down on the seat for emphasis. He indulged me but wasn't a big talker. He didn't believe in entertaining children. Sometimes we'd go to the market on the way back to his and Beba's house, sometimes to the agencia hípica to bet on horses, sometimes to play dominoes with his friends, sometimes straight home. His way of showing up involved minimal coddling. But for all his hardness, he was always surrounded by flowers. He grew orchids in the semi-exposed garage. He tended to pink and red roses, saved the pink ones for me and removed the thorns. He treated my chronic ear infections with aloe from the garden.

Kola Champagne

Buelo and I were at a chinchorro playing dominoes and drinking Kola Champagne (which is neither cola nor champagne, but a strange carbonated syrup boasting 53 grams of sugar) when he told me he had been in love more than once. Her name was Eleanor and she had worked at the university. They had an awkward courtship. He was from the country— gentle, but rough around the edges—and she was a working woman from the city. But he loved her dearly. Things took a wrong turn when he found out her brother loved men. He couldn't imagine himself as part of their family anymore.

≈

Some months after that breakup, my grandparents' story started with a, *¿cómo le puedo ayudar?* My grandmother cashed checks. She chewed gum and filed her nails down to stumps. The glass between her and him was yellow. He said something about smelling her violet perfume from here. They got married in January of 1959 and moved into a small house in Río Piedras, some 20 minutes out of Old San Juan. My mother's brother, Pablo, was born nine months from their wedding day. He was a 10-pound baby, and his birth was an all-around traumatic experience, complete with fainting and internal bleeding. So when she was in labor with my mother, she said she put herself in God's hands. She held onto the image of the Virgin of Providence hanging from her necklace and kissed it. She insisted that the apparition she then witnessed was not an effect of the teas she drank, nor the blood she lost, but a miracle. There was Providence by her bed, telling her to push. And after another 15 hours or so, my mother miraculously gave her first shriek. My grandmother named her Providencia Milagros. Providence Miracles.

≈

My grandparents' house had a metal roof. Every drizzle was a deluge. In Puerto Rico, it's hot all year. There's the dry part of the year and the wet one, and sometimes droughts in between. We grew up rationing water, as if perpetually preparing for a hurricane. I never worried when my grandmother called out to me from the sewing room where she mended clothes and listened to the radio: *Hay sequía! Lléname par de candungos, mami!* I just went out back and filled a few buckets in the slop sink.

≈

The day I wrote my first poem, I was sitting in the backyard, on the cement. My grandparents' underwear and sheets billowed above me. My grandmother, Beba, had been washing the whites. The poem was about an ant making its way around a person's body. I rhymed "temple" with "foot." "Sien." "Pie." At my mother's, the backyard was a strip of concrete lined with 3-ft tall weeds. But here, there were flowers and trees all around, and the patch of cement felt like a lily pad.

≈

On Wednesdays after school, I'd make adobo with Beba and go to the market with Buelo to pick up yucca, yams, papayas, and cuts of meat. There was a routine, a balance and simplicity to everything. Every day, the three of us ate in silence. We listened to Olga Guillot and her outdated vibrato, swatting flies intermittently. Ana the neighbor would call out from next door, *Angélica! Angélica!* And we'd stop the music. It never was about anything serious. She probably just wanted batteries or salt. When we finished eating, Buelo would go out to smoke. When he was done, he'd come back to do the dishes, get a beer, and play cards with me. The game ended when he fell asleep, after five or seven beers. Beba made me chocolate milk. I slept in their bed until my mother came to pick me up a few hours after happy hour.

≈

Living half of my life with old people meant that I never had to play with other children. Playing with children made me uncomfortable. I could spend an entire day smelling all of the Elizabeth Taylor perfumes on Beba's dresser—White Diamonds, Black Pearls, Passion, Diamonds and Rubies. I'd put on her Maja powder and try on her jewelry and the wigs she kept in boxes that looked like cookie tins. She was the kind of woman who would drench herself in Chantilly and wear coral lipstick to go to Woolworth's, regardless of her financial situation. I'd open her closet when she was in the shower and take a small album or old trinket to examine in secret and add to my collection.

Half Moon

Neither Beba nor my mother went to beauty salons. My mother's reddish-brown hair went gray in her thirties, so she'd go to her friend Lettie's to get her hair dyed Revlon burgundy every six weeks. Beba went to a woman down the street whenever her perm needed a refresh. She wore a perm until shortly after Buelo died. She didn't get wrinkles until shortly before she died. When strangers at the mall or at parties asked her about her skincare routine, she said it involved washing her face and body with unscented Dove bars, and removing makeup with Ponds cream, *y ya*. She did her nails herself.

In pictures taken from the 1950s through the 1980s, everything from her cuticles to the beginning of her nail plates, the lunulae (the Latin word for "little moon"), was silver. The rest was red. She called all nail polish Cutex, and all nail polish remover Cutex. I was supposed to know which one she meant when she asked me to fetch it for her.

Cutex was the first company to release commercial nail varnish, in the 1910s, but it wasn't until the 1920s and 30s, when movie stars like Clara Bow and Norma Shearer popularized manicures, that it became more acceptable for housewives to wear color on their nails. Leaving the little moons bare or painting them a whiteish color meant you could go longer without having to reapply. Showing the world your moons were white also meant that you didn't have to work much with your hands. But Beba worked with her hands all day. There was a weekly menu: Monday was chicken spaghetti and potatoes. Tuesday was chicken and yuca. Wednesday was beefsteak and rice. Thursday was rice and pigeon peas. Friday was chicken in Coca-Cola and yams, maybe pineapple cake. There were sauces to mix, there were rubs, there was recao. On weekends, she didn't cook, but there was always a school uniform that needed mending, always something to sweep, shoes to polish, things to disinfect.

Maybe this is why she spent so much of her downtime on the porch filing her fingernails or painting her nails. I'd sit in the rocking chair and ask stupid questions. She'd nod or shake her head and laugh, gliding the Revlon peachy pink she graduated to in her older years down her nails like she'd been doing it for centuries, layer over week-old layer.

≈

My mother and I share a skin picking disorder, dermatillomania, which is in the obsessive-compulsive spectrum. This repetitive, involuntary need to right a wrong might be linked to my mother's compulsion to immediately dispose of any trash containing chicken bones, or pull out brown bits of grass and pick up every fallen leaf from her lawn nightly, or brush her teeth so hard she loses enamel by the day. It might explain my need to immediately clean up after a party, re-write the to-do list when I've only crossed one thing out, tweeze every single ingrown hair on my bikini line. We pick at our cuticles until we bleed while driving, watching TV, talking on the phone, thinking. When I saw her ridged yet painted nailbeds, surrounded by rawness, on all the fingers wrapped around the steering wheel, I asked her, ashamed for her, why she would hurt herself like that. *Imítame en lo bueno*, she'd say. When I first noticed my own mangled nail ridges in high school, I had no idea how they got there.

Secreto

Before my grandmother died, she left each of her three granddaughters a little bit of money and one of her gemstone bee pins. I lost mine, a deep sapphire one, the first time I wore it. I got all her pictures, too, because she knew I had been sneaking into her closet all those years, much like I had been sneaking into my mother's hoarding room. She left my mother and uncle the house, which they sold for pennies. My mother sounded relieved. *The past is the past*, she said.

≈

She has never said as much, but I believe the course of my mother's life changed during her first year at university. A man, probably another student, stalked her for several weeks. He followed her to the parking lot one day and waited until she had gotten into her car before he ran over to it and rubbed his penis on her window. She never went back. I'm sure there is something missing from this story, but there are some things she has kept secret despite her penchant for over-sharing. All I know is that a few months passed, and Buelo helped her get a job as a secretary at a hospital.

≈

Secrets are our family members, too. One day a year, my grandmother would lock herself in her room and mourn something. My mother won't tell me she is going on a trip until the day before. *Don't tell your father I'm traveling*, she'd say 20 years after their divorce. My uncle won't tell my mother how much he makes, or when he has a new girlfriend, or when his daughter, my mother's niece, is getting married. My mother doesn't know I've had a tattoo for a decade. She and her brother meet each other for a drink every week, listen to jazz piano, but she doesn't know where he'll sleep that night.

You know Beba loved him more than me. They would've never let me study in Mayaguez. I wasn't a man. Those were different times. You're lucky, she said into her glass this one time I joined them for a drink over holiday break after I had left home. *Lucky*, I say, as my uncle passes me an envelope with money for utilities under the table. *Don't tell your mother*, he mouths to me as she orders another drink.

II. Hurricane San Ciprián

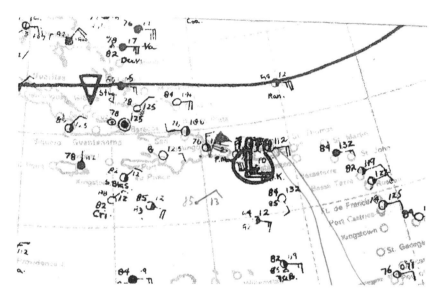

Weather map of Hurricane San Ciprián right over Puerto Rico on September 27, 1932.

Paternal Family Tree

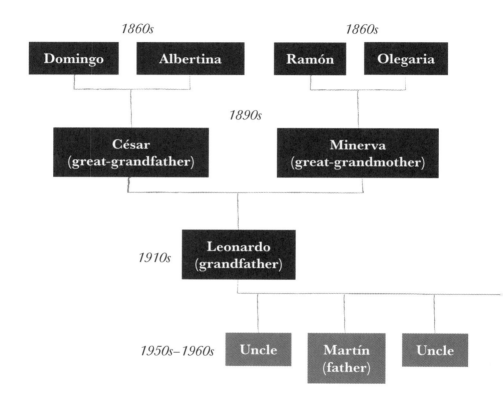

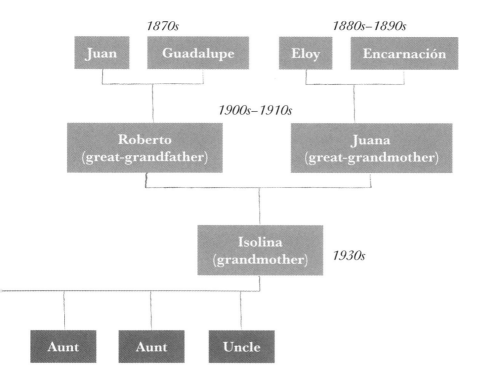

Historical Notes

After the invasion in 1898, Puerto Rico was submitted to U.S. military rule and governed by officials appointed by the States.

≈

Around 80% percent of the population was illiterate at the end of Spanish rule on the island. Only 1% of adults on the island had received lower secondary education at the time. Around the time my grandmother Isolina left school, that number had only increased by 15%.

≈

From an unmailed letter written in 1931 (he later stated it was a "playful composition written entirely for [his] own diversion") by Cornelius Rhodes, a Rockefeller Institute pathologist conducting research in the San Juan Presbyterian Hospital, after his car was vandalized:

> I can get a damn fine job here and am tempted to take it. It would be ideal except for the Porto Ricans. They are beyond doubt the dirtiest, laziest, most degenerate and thievish race of men ever inhabiting this sphere. It makes you sick to inhabit the same island with them. They are even lower than Italians. What the island needs is not public health work but a tidal wave or something to totally exterminate the population. It might then be livable. I have done my best to further the process of extermination by killing off 8 and transplanting cancer into several more.

It was signed, "Dusty."

≈

In 1937, the island enacted Law 116, which instituted a population control program designed to catalyze "economic growth" and respond to "depression-era unemployment." Strategies used to push poor women into getting tubal ligations included door-to-door visits by health workers, financial incentives, and employer favoritism. These strategies limited informed consent to the point that many women who underwent the operation did not know that tubal ligation would leave them permanently sterile. The law was repealed in 1960. Despite this, and in part due to the high cost of the birth control pill Enovid ($11 a month in 1960), tubal ligations were pervasive well into the 1970s. The U.S Department of Health, Education, and Welfare reported that by 1976, over 37 percent of women of childbearing age in Puerto Rico had been sterilized.)

≈

In 1938, the Democratic Popular Party, which is still favored by Puerto Ricans in most elections, was founded by Luis Muñoz Marín. Their slogan was "Bread, Land, and Liberty."

≈

The party favored the island's independence in its initial stages, but went on to lean toward the middle, contributing to the status quo.

≈

On February 23, 1936, nationalists Hiram Rosado and Elias Beauchamp killed the island's police chief. This was in response to a police-led massacre at the University of Puerto Rico in Río Piedras. Both men were captured and shot to death.

≈

On July 23 of the same year, Nationalist Party leader Pedro Albizu Campos, along with several other nationalist leaders, were sentenced to a federal prison in Atlanta, Georgia after being charged with sedition. He was released 11 years later.

≈

Campos was jailed again in 1950, and again later that year for being linked to Oscar Collazo and Griselio Torresola's failed attack on Harry S. Truman. That time he was sentenced to 80 years in prison. Campos was pardoned in 1953 by the then governor of the newly coined "free associated state," Muñoz Marín. But his pardon was revoked after Lolita Lebrón, Rafael Cancel, Irvin Flores, and Andrés Figeroa opened fire at the U.S. House of Representatives in D.C. in 1954, wounding five Congressmen. They were sentenced to 50 years imprisonment.

César

My father's father
lost his father
before a mudslide,
or rather,
due to a self-inflicted gunshot wound
before a mudslide.

My father's father
was a child
when his father killed himself.

At the family movie theater,
the first one in town,
in the mountains of Corozal,
he must have seen the future:

the pooling rain,
the broken glass,
the missing gold,

and decided he was done
climbing that mountain.

If all the storms from before
hadn't cut through the island
east to west,
causing the earth to erode,
maybe my father's father
would have seen his father love him
and maybe even loved my father's mother more.

Maybe my own father would have loved my mother more,
maybe even loved himself,
had his father's father not cut through his wife
hip to hip,
navel to groin,
eroding all in his wake
seven times too many, only
to run off course.

Hurricane San Ciprián

On September 26, 1932, four years after Hurricane San Felipe II, San Ciprián hit Puerto Rico after crossing St. Maarten, Anguilla, and the Virgin Islands as a Category 3. It took seven hours for the storm, with winds of up to 120 mph at landfall, to cross the island, after which it headed on westward until it dissipated on October 3. Its east-to-west path, a trajectory that wouldn't repeat itself until Hurricane Georges in 1998, guaranteed destruction across most of the 78 municipalities.

≈

Around 250 people died, as well as more than 400,000 livestock. More than 70,000 families saw their houses destroyed or partially destroyed. Hundreds of houses were blown away in the town of Río Piedras alone. Most of the citrus crops were destroyed. The total cost of the damage was around 30 million dollars (close to $655 million by today's standards), in a time when the island was still recovering from losses suffered during San Felipe II in 1928.

≈

"Que hoy día, un poquito de dolor no es tanto. Que aprendamos. Que cojamos esa enseñanza. Que si no tenemos luz, que demos gracias a Dios; que, si no tenemos buen pan, que demos gracias a Dios porque estamos con vida."

"That nowadays, a little bit of pain isn't so bad. That we learn. That we learn that lesson. That if we have no power, to thank God; that, if we have no good bread, we thank God that we are alive."

—Isolina "Sol" Gómez Aponte, 87-year-old San Ciprián survivor, when asked by a *Nuevo Día* reporter about what she would tell her fellow Puerto Ricans as they waited for Hurricane María, September 19, 2017.

Neil Armstrong

A father is a legend. He can be told in a number of ways. He is there to explain something that happened. The fathers in this story are Odysseus, icons for leaving and cunning. My father's father lost his father to suicide. My father's father was a gallivanting joker. I wonder if my father has grown to believe his stories.

What I knew of my father's parents came to me from his tall tales, bits and pieces from overheard conversations, and my uncle's poems. What I thought was true was this:

My great-grandfather owned one of the first movie theaters in the town of Corozal. Right around the beginning of the Depression, his earnings plummeted. He shot himself.

His son, my grandfather, married my grandmother when he was 32 and she was 15 or 16. An orphan, she stopped going to school after the fifth grade to make money for herself and her wheelchair-bound brother. Her father had been a cobbler. The mother wasn't around. When she met my grandfather, she may have been working as a shop girl and living in her aunt's hostel in Santurce. She had six children—four boys and two girls—by the time she was in her mid-twenties. My father was the second or third oldest son.

I rarely saw her smile except for when she danced or sang. She called my grandfather by his surname and drew girlish flowers on napkins.

≈

My father said she rarely left the house when he and his siblings were growing up, that her closest friends were nuns who sent her messages clipped to clotheslines and stopped by to watch TV. When Neil Armstrong walked on the moon, the nuns were there, sitting among the children.

≈

Six children: the aspiring actor, the car salesman, the poet, the two secretaries, my father, the altar boy.

≈

My uncle, the poet, writes, *make me coffee lovingly, so we don't have to say I love you.*

≈

I avoided my father's hugs after he called my breasts "tetas," after I realized he wasn't a safe harbor like in the movies. We'd visit his parents' house—green, brown, and plastic, with green and white tiles, and faux-linen wallpaper—every other court-ordered Sunday and I'd wait for the physical assessment from my grandfather and my dad. *You're getting a little fat, you're too thin, look at those legs, big hams like your mother's, how is she, by the way. You'll have an amazing body when you're older.* And wait until I was excused.

≈

Like in an epic poem, the arbitrary nature of the gods reigned in my father's house. He'd have me sit in front of a plate of pink beans for hours to prove a point I didn't understand. There were social experiments. There were games designed to make my siblings and me lose. Now I picture his mother's downturned mouth, her strong knobby hands, her small, fragile frame, his father's suggestive jokes, the crosses hanging in every room, my father as a boy, in church, the answer "because," and who he might have been before the weight of his history fell on him. I was raised to be on the defense. Always with an emergency backpack under my bed, always holding on to comebacks in case of a surprise attack, always expecting a sort of violence from every man. I was spared from his belt, but I wasn't sure why.

César, Again

My paternal great-grandfather César and I almost shared a birthday. We may have if I hadn't wrapped the umbilical cord around my neck three times or tried to leave my mother's birth canal ass-first when she went into labor, which delayed things by a couple of days. I still can't sleep unless I'm twisting myself into uncomfortable positions. People born that week in January are, according to my old copy of *The Secret Language of Birthdays*, "chaotic," "difficult," "eruptive," "exciting," "entertaining," and "lighthearted," on any given day. Under the advice section for those born on January 17 it reads, "RELINQUISHING CONTROL CAN FREE YOU."

César was born on January 17, 1895, to Domingo and Albertina, in Carolina, a municipality now also referred to as the "Tierra de Gigantes" due to it being the birthplace of the tallest Puerto Rican on record, Felipe Birriel (7'11), and the late poet Julia de Burgos (1914–1953). Two months after César was born, the Lumière brothers released what is incorrectly considered to be the first movie ever made, "Workers Leaving the Lumière Factory." When my father told me César had owned the first movie theater in his town, I didn't question it.

Domingo, César's father, died of tuberculosis on New Year's Eve, 1897. The Spanish American War wouldn't happen for another 16 months, so Puerto Rico was still a province of Spain.

César was two years old and the youngest of three sons when his father died. He was three years old when the U.S. flag replaced the Spanish one on every school, hospital, and government building. According to a 1917 World War I registration card I found on the internet, César, a government clerk at 22, claimed to be exempt from military service because he was providing for his widowed mother. His weight and height are registered as, "regular." His eyes and hair were brown. He was white.

That same year, in December, he married my great-grandmother Minerva in Corozal, a mountainous town in the Cordillera Central that is prone to mudslides and floods due to the many rivers running through it. The name "Corozal" comes from "corozo," a type of palm tree that thrives there.

Minerva's name means "of the mind." She was the eldest of five sisters, all born two years apart. Minerva, Rosario, Mercedes, Rosaura, Ramona.

My grandfather Leonardo was born a year after César and Minerva got married, seven months after Albertina, César's long-widowed mother, died. Then five other kids were born. Then, around 4:00 p.m. on his 33rd birthday, César died. Nowhere on the death certificate I found (again on the internet) does it say he owned anything, much less a movie theater. His occupation is listed as being "empleado," "employee"—no company, no store. If he did own a theater, I couldn't find a record confirming it. As far as I can remember, my father was the only person to tell me this story. I'm not sure if this was something he was told as a child, or made up and ended up believing. Things that are, without question, true, are that the first movie ever made was "Roundhay Garden Scene" by Louis Le Prince in 1888, and that on January 17, 1927, Eartha Kitt was born in South Carolina, *The Scarlet Letter* with Lillian Gish was showing in theaters, it was a Monday, and it was the day my great-grandfather César shot a bullet into his brain.

Minerva was five months pregnant when César died. She went on to outlive at least two of her children and died two years before I was born. I have one picture of her. She looks about 35, the age I am now. If she was in fact 35, her husband would die a couple of years later. She has the eyes of someone hollowing out, a downturned mouth, an avian nose. She poses with a bunch of dark roses in her hands. She keeps them away from her chest like she's saying, *is this what you want?*

Isolina

My paternal grandmother Isolina's parents were named Roberto and Juana. He was a traveling cobbler who died in his late thirties from tuberculosis. Juana, who was raised in Yauco, and Roberto got together when she was a teenager. Neither she nor her parents could read or write. Her father, Roberto, was a farmworker. Census documents state that he planted and harvested "frutos menores," "minor fruit." I am not sure what happened to Juana, except she wasn't in Isolina's life after the latter turned 10. There was a woman with Juana's name and age and a husband who wasn't Roberto who died from an infection during childbirth a few blocks away from my great-grandfather. Roberto's death certificate from 1944 lists him as single.

I think Isolina was given a place to stay by an aunt who owned a hostel in Santurce, and there was something strange about her being made to sleep in the room of a woman who had hung herself there. Or so my father told me.

≈

I don't remember hugging my grandmother. I remember not feeling at home in her gaze. My cousins' adoration for her and my grandfather is at odds with my experience of their home. I saw them every other Sunday. I was a visitor. When in front of them I couldn't think of things to say.

My father often called attention to the power imbalance in his parents' relationship. The way Isolina called Leonardo, my grandfather, by his surname, because she was a child when she married him. My father made excuses for her seriousness, her aloofness, but also seemed to begrudge it. It must have been odd to have been raised by someone whose life was coopted at a young age by marriage and children. To be curious, empathetic, and smart about a parent's experience, but also need unabashed, warm love.

I know this because I also needed it. I know my parents couldn't give it in the way they wanted to. But understanding something doesn't help one make peace with it. It makes the attainment of the missing thing all the more urgent. I can uncover my parents' history, evaluate their intentions, forgive them, level with them. But my life will always be the undoing of the idea, the feeling that I am not a good enough reason to get healthy.

≈

My twin cousins and I were dropped off at our grandparents' one day. Our parents were working and we were on summer break. Isolina was tired, so she suggested that we play doctor and pretend she was the patient. My cousins and I went into caretaker mode, gathered gauze, tweezers, a comb, cotton balls, and Agua Maravilla, which cures most ailments. We took turns running the cotton balls we'd soaked in the witch hazel up and down her arms. Isolina would go, *Ouch! Help me, doctor*, and smile with her eyes closed when the cotton touched her skin.

Farms in the hills of Corozal circa 1941.

Materials

When I was eight, my uncle gifted me a book of poems he wrote. Some members of our family were featured in it. He gave away details in a gentle and economical way that I wish I could match. I learned the name of Isolina's father reading it. I learned that his fingernails were dirty, that he loved baseball and a good drink and a jukebox. He sang, like his daughter. He fixed shoes. I wish I knew what his face looked like when he looked at my grandmother, or when he replaced a sole by a tiny oil lamp. I learned he walked to visit a woman at the Princesa prison in secondhand shoes. I learned that the ocean was deeper then, and that the woman he visited left her ghost in a rented room after she was released. That woman may or may not have been my great-grandmother. My grandmother may or may not have stayed in that room. But I am afraid to ask any more.

In my uncle's poem about my grandfather, I met an entirely different younger Leonardo than the one I made up. My uncle's version was whimsical, hardworking, a bedtime story provider, as dreamy and wholesome as a Sunday.

Velveeta

The morning before I sang at the governor's Christmas concert, I ate half a tray of sandwiches de mezcla.[1] They'd been sitting out overnight. Isolina had made them for my cousins and me. We had had a sleepover at her house, which was out of the ordinary. In the morning there were seven sandwiches left, and I must have been nervous because I ate all of them over the course of four hours.

My dad picked me up with my stepmom. She was eight months pregnant and couldn't sit without spreading her legs. On the drive to Old San Juan, he looked down at her stomach and told her to close them, because *that's how you got knocked up.*

She looked back at me like she was sorry and I turned up the volume on my Discman. I listened to Ben Kweller sing about how having sex was like eating spaghetti.

The concert was televised. The lights were hot and white. In the middle of "Little Drummer Boy," the space between the audience and me became a kaleidoscope. I made my way down the choral risers as daintily as I could and ran to the bathroom, past the governor, past my principal, and past a couple of senators, with my hand over my mouth as if it could stop anything. The toilet, when I got to it, was white and beige marble. I vomited until there was only bile, and then sat on the floor listening to another girl sing my solo. *I played my best for him pa rum pum pum pum, then he smiled at me pa rum pum pum pum, me and my drum.*

---

[2] To make sandwiches de mezcla, or Puerto Rican spread, you need a can of Spam, a can of pimentos, and a block of Velveeta. Some people like to add a little mayonnaise. Throw the ingredients in a food processor and blend until it achieves a paste-like consistency. Refrigerate for a few minutes. Spread only on Wonder Bread or potato bread. Get rid of the crusts and cut diagonally, into triangles.

Vendepatria

Vendepatria. Pitiyanqui. Bocabajo. Homelandseller. Little Yankee lover. Little oligarch. If I removed my headphones in the car, I could hear my father say these words from time to time. Directed at a politician on a billboard. Directed at a fast-food franchise. Directed, sometimes, at my stepbrother and me.

Granted, like two good little colonized teenagers in the early aughts, we wore spikes and Converse sneakers and listened to Operation Ivy. I wore long black skirts and turtlenecks in 90-degree weather, though that had more to do with a fear of people's perception of my body than anything else (it was also a direct response to my father's suggestion that I show more skin and smile). We sporadically used English in conversations with our friends, and had a predilection for movies, television, and trends that were meant to belong to kids growing up in the U.S. This wasn't, I don't think, a conscious rejection of our culture, though it may have seemed that way to my father. I'm sure he would've liked us to have read more Mayra Santos and less Bukowski, to have listened to more Pablo Casals and less Rage Against the Machine. I wish I had, too.

As long as I'd known him, he was staunchly pro-independence. The Partido Independentista Puertorriqueño was something my father and mother's families had in common, before and after they went their separate ways. Our flags had the right shade of sky blue. We went to the *Claridad* festival every year. My parents' second date was a Silvio Rodríguez concert. One of my father's favorite things about my mother was my Buelo and his siblings' involvement in the Nationalist Party. The fact that my great-aunt María's husband went to jail for political reasons added to my mother's value as a spouse. Beba had a thing for Fidel Castro even though his fingernails were too long. I had Che Guevara's face on a couple of t-shirts and even knew who he was.

To my father, however, speaking English well was just as important as knowing the revolutionary version of our national anthem: "Wake up from that dream, for it's time to fight." To defeat the enemy, you have to speak their language. Pedro Albizu Campos and Derek Walcott knew this. When Pedro was alive, though, there were no Wendy's drive-thrus in Guaynabo, or LiveJournals. So you can see how things got murky.

III. Hurricane Hugo

Satellite image of Hurricane Hugo over Puerto Rico on September 18, 1989.

Family Tree

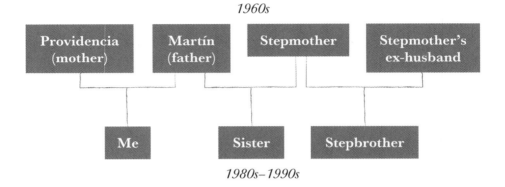

1960s

Providencia (mother) — Martín (father) — Stepmother — Stepmother's ex-husband

Me — Sister — Stepbrother

1980s–1990s

Historical Notes

In October of 1950, Nationalists Raimundo Díaz Pacheco, Domingo Hiraldo, Carlos Hiraldo, Manuel Torres, and Gregorio Hernández attempted to assassinate Governor Luis Muñoz Marín. Fortaleza guards killed all but Gregorio Hernández, who was badly injured.

≈

Earlier that same year, Harry S. Truman signed Public Act 600, which allowed Puerto Ricans to draft their own constitution. In 1952, voters approved the latter in a referendum, and the island was "upgraded" from protectorate to commonwealth. It remained a territory of the United States and was still treated as a colony.

≈

The institution of the Commonwealth of Puerto Rico freed the United States from reporting on the status of the island to the United Nations Decolonization Committee.

≈

In 1953, around 70,000 Puerto Ricans emigrated to New York, New Jersey, and Florida.

≈

In 1956, the first large-scale human trial of the birth control pill was launched in a public housing project in Puerto Rico. The dosage was much higher than what is now administered. By 1964, thousands of women had been given several different versions. While some dropped out of the trial due to side effects including dizziness, nausea, and even bleeding irregularities leading to hospitalization, many Puerto Rican women continued to participate in the experiment.

≈

In 1962, Rita Moreno won an Oscar for her portrayal of Anita, the funny friend who loved Manhattan, in *West Side Story*.

≈

In 1965, Pedro Albizu Campos, leader of the Nationalist Party, died shortly after being pardoned by Muñoz Marín and released from La Princesa prison, where he was subjected to radiation experiments. The guards there deemed him "king of the towels," as he used to tie them around his head to try to protect himself from exposure to radiation.

≈

On July 23, 1967, Puerto Ricans had the first plebiscite on the political status of the island. These were the results:
Commonwealth: 60.4 percent
Statehood: 39 percent
Independence: less than 1 percent

≈

Prior to the plebiscite that year, the Partido Estadistas Unidos (United Statehooders Party) was founded by Luis A. Ferré to campaign for statehood.

≈

In 1968, Luis A. Ferré was elected governor with 43.6 percent of the vote. His slogan was "Esto tiene que cambiar." "This must change."

≈

In 1970, the U.S. Navy took over almost all of Culebra, a Puerto Rican municipality off the northeastern coast of the island, for bombing practices.

≈

In 1971, the Puerto Rican Socialist Party was founded by Juan Mari Brás.

≈

A couple of years later, the Fuerzas Armadas de Liberación Nacional (Armed Forces of National Liberation), or FALN, a militant Marxist nationalist group from Puerto Rico, set off a bomb at Fraunces Tavern in New York City, killing 4 and injuring 50. They claimed responsibility for that and more than 100 other bombings in the United States.

≈

In November of 1976, Carlos Romero Barceló was elected governor with 48.3 percent of the vote.

≈

That same year, section 936 of the United States Internal Revenue Tax Code, which granted tax breaks to American companies that made profits in U.S. territories, was implemented. Tens of thousands of Puerto Ricans ended up being employed by Section 936 companies, mostly pharmaceutical.

≈

On July 25, 1978, Carlos Enrique Soto Arriví and Arnaldo Darío Rosado Torres, 18 and 24, respectively, along with an undercover cop posing as a pro-independence group member, took a taxi driver hostage and drove to Cerro Maravilla, the island's 4th highest peak. Carlos and Arnaldo intended, according to the authorities, to set fire to two communication towers to protest the incarceration of nationalists involved in the assassination attempts and shootings that took place in the early 1950s. The two men were ambushed, beaten, and killed by police officers. Governor Romero Barceló and other high-ranking officials were later accused of planning and covering up the murders.

≈

In 1981, the Boricua Popular Army (also known as the "macheteros," the "machete wielders") blew up 11 National Guard jet fighters in San Juan.

≈

In 1996, President Bill Clinton signed legislation to phase out Section 936 of the tax code over a 10-year period, ending in 2006.

I

Hurricane Hugo
Guaynabo
September 18, 1989

did you wonder
as he boarded up the windows
and my fever spiked
why holding me close
didn't stop the wailing

      did you cry, too,
      and did he hold us
      as the wind slammed palm trees
      into our house

            it must have looked like a pink flower
            at the center of a locust swarm

      (27 years later
      a farmer would tell me
      i wouldn't be prone
      to ear infections
      like the one i had that day
      if you had breastfed me)

do you think he wanted out
when he saw them cut you open

or was it when he saw you couldn't handle
giving me a bath

or was it even earlier
when you wouldn't
get on your knees

or did you feel it for the first time
alone with me
in that hallway,
the safest place in our house
during the hurricane

did you know then
that was the way
it always would be
all the other times
the sea rushed
through the door gaps

(33 years later
2,590 kilometers away
mine would be the only dry eye
in the flooded basement
I shared with three other women)

did you wonder
as you rocked me sleepless
through the ache
in indefinite darkness
what good a storm window was
when the rain came from inside

Hurricane Hugo

Hurricane Hugo formed in Cape Verde, off the western coast of Africa, on September 13, 1989. Five days later, it made landfall in Vieques as a Category 3—almost 4—storm, with winds averaging at 130 mph. At its strongest, there were wind gusts of up to 170 mph, according to the anemometer on a ship in the harbor at Culebra.

≈

Hurricane force winds in eastern Puerto Rico lasted about four hours, their intensity peaking between 8:00 and 9:00 a.m. The storm continued moving northwest, with the eye passing about 20 miles north of the capital, San Juan.

≈

While the western and southern parts of the island suffered minimal to no damage, the eastern part of Puerto Rico, including Culebra and Vieques, were deeply affected. Around 80 percent of houses were either damaged or destroyed.

≈

"There were boats buried in the mountains. They flew across the streets, and the wind threw them at the mountains. The pressure of the wind and the tide dragged a great amount of boats, and the ones that weren't taken out of the bay, sank. There were dozens and dozens."

"We would share food, have potlucks, shared the food we had, and whoever had a generator would share with a neighbor, despite it being risky...people sitting in their patios, cooling off [...]" —Former Secretary of Justice, Hector Rivera Cruz, a few days before Hurricane

María, remembering Hurricane Hugo in an interview for *Primera Hora* (September 2017).

≈

The power came back on a month later.

Things My Father Has Been

My father always said that he wished he had married a redheaded Communist Russian with liquor on her breath, or an ex-nun. He had wanted a truckload of daughters. Instead, he had my sister and me with two different women and drove a red Pathfinder.

≈

I'm not sure where or when his issues with women started, but it led him to quit the priesthood and marry around four times. I write "around" because there are things about him that might never be revealed to me.

≈

There was a young teacher he may have married in Niagara Falls. She may have cheated on him with a Dominican taxi driver. There was a Belgian woman with big tits who insisted on calling him Marcello because his Spanish name, Martín, was not sophisticated enough, or so he told me once. There was an actor, my sister's mother, and there was the freckled secretary with big legs who was my mother. When I ask her why she married him, she always starts her story by saying she was young.

≈

They met shortly after he returned to the island from an attempt at graduate school in the States, where his second marriage hadn't worked out. He never admitted to not completing his degree. His aunt and my mother both worked at the Industrial Hospital in San Juan. The aunt introduced her to my father in his parents' house, where he was living at the time. It was December of 1982.

≈

A few days before Christmas, they went to a holiday party at the hospital.

$$\approx$$

Things my father has been: altar boy, seminarian, history teacher, consultant, talent scout, ad man, goji berries salesman, weight loss pills salesman, graphic designer, entrepreneur, producer, cinematographer, filmmaker, headhunter.

The Man You Don't Understand
Sings Himself to Sleep

The moon is sweet and silver,
keeps my worries in a crater,
deep in dust and glitter,
when the heels go, clack-clack-clack,
and the swishing tulle goes, hush,
and the clock strikes twelve, then one.

She goes, *sleep, my honey bear,*
and beats my nightmares soft,
casts a shadow on the girl
hanging from the roof.

She goes, *does it swell your chest,*
my littlest of lambs,
when I make her disappear
and it's just us nightingales
singing songs like wounds.

Carve all your hopes and fears
into my downturned cheek.
Only I can understand
my baby's fever dreams.

The moon is fair and sexy:
When the heels go, clack-clack-clack,
and the swishing tulle goes, hush,
and the clock strikes twelve, then one,

and I'm sweating through my sheets,
she fits my fist inside her mouth,
a cave made out of bones,
meant for no one else
but me.

My Mother Cries in Her Underwear

When I was 16, my father got us a bottle of white wine and told me that when they first met, all he wanted to do with my mother was get in her pants, but she wouldn't put out.

≈

Three months after meeting, he took her hand on the way to a friend's, and asked her for it. They had a modest party at her parents' and decided on a wedding ring budget—no more than $600 for both. Hers was $400; his, $200. They were married in July.

≈

I was two when my father met my mother at a restaurant to tell her that he needed time away from her. She had gotten too fat and refused to dye her hair.

≈

Two months later, the pediatrician was giving me a booster shot when she told my mother she had seen him with a brunette. Two-and-a-half months later, he was on the cover of a magazine, marrying an actor with baby's breath in her hair. They had met during a commercial shoot he directed: she and her famous mother played congas shaped like giant adobo bottles.

≈

One of my earliest memories is of the day after he left. I was two. She and I were sitting on her bed and she told me my father would not live with us anymore. Then we went to Plaza Las Américas and she bought me clothes I would outgrow a couple of weeks later. At the Sears perfume counter, I informed her that I wouldn't love him.

≈

In another memory, my mother cries in her underwear. She is red all over. I've gotten out of my crib and followed the screaming into the living room. He was pointing at her. I asked him to stop yelling. He pointed at me. Then, *You. You shut the fuck up*.

≈

I said my first word at 5 months. It was "Beba." Then there was "mama." Then there was "papa." Then there was "nena." Then there was "agua." Grandma, Mama, Papa, Girl, Water.

Damage in Culebra, Puerto Rico, on September 18, 1989.

Language

Beba told me that the name I gave her
was plucked from the stratus cloud where language lives,
that sounds there bounce off each other all day and night
until we pick them out with flash-lightning fingers
so fast that we don't even notice
our hands bringing them to our mouths.

Mija

Over my last week in the womb, I got into a sitting position and wrapped the umbilical cord around my neck, making it impossible for my mother to push me out without killing us both. She would relay this to people with great pride, reminding them that babies who are difficult to birth are smarter.

≈

My mother had lost a baby in February, about a week before her 26th birthday. She still calls him my brother. Alejandro. By April, she was pregnant with me. My father liked the name Ninotchka, the name of his favorite Chekov character and the title of a movie starring Greta Garbo. In it she played a Russian envoy who falls in love with a Parisian dandy and champagne. An old poster for the movie informs us that her first glass opened up a new life for her. Another swears, "Garbo Laughs!" and orders us to "[Not] Pronounce It—See It!" My mother wanted to name me after an Italian actress. She thought she was the most beautiful girl in the world. The name, derived from the Latin "claudus," means "lame, crippled."

≈

My parents got into a fight about body piercings in the delivery room. She wanted me to wear earrings. He said we weren't Yoruba people. She called him a racist. He left the room to pace around. In the 1980s it was still customary to offer free ear piercings to newborn girls as part of the birth package. Beba, who had been praying to all sorts of virgins in the waiting area, gave the nurse a pair of diamond earrings she had been saving for me behind my father's back. All my life, whenever she saw me without earrings, it was a tragedy. *You are a lady, mija. You are breaking my heart looking like that.*

≈

The day of the hurricane, my father filled the tub with water, brought in the ficus trees we had in our semi-exposed garage, and raided the supermarket at the last minute for cans of Vienna sausages, corned beef, soup, soursop juice, and corn.

≈

Early in the morning my mother and I lay down in the hallway as he moved his books away from the windows. When the wind picked up, he had us hide in his office, and we all sat on the floor, under his big metal desk, for three hours. The next day he went out and bought what he said was the last generator in Guaynabo.

≈

My ear infection started the night before the hurricane. I was one year old. I was often sick. I cried through the storm and the days after that. A doctor said that I'd need a myringotomy, to have these tiny tubes inserted in my eardrums, to prevent hearing loss. The infection was almost too advanced. My mother didn't like the idea of anyone putting tubes in me, so she opted for a month-long course of antibiotics, which worked.

Agua

In kindergarten, I was still exclusively drinking from bottles. I had never pet a dog or eaten a meal in our dining room. I wasn't potty trained. I was scared of dogs, pools, toilets, and showers. I was comfortable with television, powdered milk, chicken nugget breading, fruit cocktail, and waiting for someone to pick me up from school.

The first time I took a shower was shortly after the court decided I'd stay at my father's once a week. My stepmother told him to leave the bathroom, helped me out of my clothes, and held my hand as I screamed under perfectly tepid water. She looked me straight in the eyes and said, *you're fine, you're fine, water won't kill you.*

Mother Scar

My grandmother told me it was the "mother scar," and that everyone who got the chicken pox had one, the mark from the biggest blister. My grandmother would say a lot of things, so I didn't believe her. I sat in the tub, in the oatmeal bath in the pink bathroom with the sliding mirrors, ruined. I didn't believe her, but I loved her, because she gave me a glass bell with my name on it that I was to ring whenever I itched. And she'd come into the room with Caladryl and dab it on my blisters. People kiss the scar on my left breast because they can't see it.

Keepsakes

No one was allowed in my mother's hoarding room. Not even me, her only child. It used to be my father's office. After he left, my mother started to compulsively buy striped button-downs, fish figurines (she is a Pisces), and miniature elephants (for good luck). She began to amass jewelry boxes (lacquered wood, porcelain, plastic) and carved soaps like they were provisions for bunker life after a nuclear apocalypse. And she stored everything in that room.

≈

My bedroom was right across from it when I was young. I would try to sneak in when I knew she was there, but she would lock the door from within if she heard me approach it. One summer, during school break, she let me stay home alone while she went to work. I eventually figured out where she kept the key (a small cardboard box in her medicine cabinet). The moment I realized I had access to this part of my mother, I felt a surge of energy so great that the shame of infringement didn't really hit until I wrote this.

≈

I went through the rows of identical shirts with the tags still on, the boxes of unused shoes, the old photo albums, my father's college textbooks, the books he used to teach with back when he had a job, the copies of *The Joy of Sex* he later told me he had made my mother read, abandoned party dresses, dusty bottles of Cutty Sark, the fish, the tiny soaps, an old metal desk with my mother's will and journals, wrapping paper. There was a single pathway, about six inches wide, from the door to the end of the room, winding around all the stuff.

≈

When I'd go back home for my yearly visit before I stopped going altogether, I tried to get her to clean the room with me, but she refused, even though she had known for a decade that I knew what she hid there. Around eight years ago, when the room was filled to capacity, floor-to-ceiling, wall-to-wall, she moved on to filling the rest of the house. Save for a small frying pan, an old pot, a rusty knife, and a few forks, she doesn't own any cookware, but she had dozens of tiny thimbles covering all the counters.

≈

She makes her cream cheese and canned chicken dip on the washing machine and eats the concoction with crackers in bed. We always ate our food in our respective beds, but for a while there was nowhere else to go. My old bathroom was a shoe closet that happened to have a broken toilet in it. The coffee table in the living room was a shrine to the nameless families in clearance picture frames from Marshalls. We had our drinks and conversation on the floor.

≈

She eventually stopped locking the door to the room. She doesn't have visitors. I would wait until the pill knocked her out or when she was in the shower to go in and take something—a locket, an old photo of hers or my grandma's, a pair of sandals (we wear the same size). I don't know if she noticed that things went missing, but she has never mentioned it.

IV. Hurricane Georges

Satellite image of Hurricane Georges making landfall on Puerto Rico on September 21, 1998.

Historical Notes

In 1993, Spanish and English were declared the official languages of Puerto Rico, one year after Pedro Roselló was elected governor and two years after the island received Spain's Asturias Award for declaring Spanish the official language.

≈

Also in 1993, 48.6 percent of Puerto Ricans voted in favor of remaining a commonwealth in a referendum.

≈

In 1994, Juan Mari Brás was the first person to renounce his U.S. citizenship for Puerto Rican citizenship.

≈

Another non-binding referendum took place in 1998. Puerto Rican voters were given five choices that time: remaining a commonwealth, entering into a "free association" with the U.S. that would be somewhere between commonwealth and independence, becoming a state, declaring independence, or none of the above. "None of the above" obtained the majority of votes: 50.30 percent.

≈

In 1999, two U.S. Navy jets dropped bombs over the municipality-island of Vieques during a training exercise. One civilian was killed and four others were injured. Protesters then started occupying the bombing range on the island. In the previous year alone, 7,300 shells had been fired, creating 14,600 sonic booms.

≈

In April of 2001, the Navy resumed bombing exercises, and didn't leave until 2003. Since then, the bombing range has simultaneously become a federal wildlife refuge and a Superfund site, barred off for cleanup by the EPA.

≈

Since the 1940s, Vieques's population has been exposed to napalm, toxic levels of arsenic, depleted uranium, mercury, and a host of other heavy metals, making their cancer rates disproportionately higher than that of mainland PR. As of 2019, the U.S. Navy anticipates cleanup on land and underwater will not be completed for another 20 years.

≈

In 2002, Telemundo was purchased by NBC for $2.7 billion.

≈

The lack of population growth in the early 2000s, drops in employment, three years of budget deficits brought on by cash flow mismanagement and the phase-out of Section 936 of the Internal Revenue Code, which allowed for U.S. corporations operating in PR to get significant tax credits, among other reasons, resulted in a $740 million deficit in public funds in the 2005–2006 fiscal year. This led to a two-week shutdown, leaving a quarter of a million public employees without pay or access to services other than the police and hospitals.

Providencia

Hurricane Georges
Guaynabo
September 21, 1998

I learned from you
that Operation is a game best played
by the light of the Virgin Mary candle
from the dollar store
while sharing the last cold can
of soursop juice.

You were never more my mother
than during a blackout,
when you let me win at a musty board game
and sleep on the right side of your bed,
half cave,
half anchored sailboat
in high tide.

That night in September you asked me
to name the types of clouds
as we drifted:
Cumul-
    us
Strat-
    us

Cirr-
        us
and I heard you smile in the dark.

I fell asleep
to the whir of your breath
half happy,
half scared of
the surge.

Hurricane Georges

Hurricane Georges, the first to cross the entirety of Puerto Rico since San Ciprián in 1932, formed on September 15, 1998, 300 miles southwest of the Cape Verde Islands. It strengthened to a Category 3 at landfall in Puerto Rico, on September 21. It caused 10- to 20-ft storm surges and dumped up to 30 inches of water. Tornadoes were reported. Initially carrying sustained winds of 115 mph while it was over Puerto Rico, it weakened to a Category 2 as it crossed the western part of the island and left around 1:00 am the following morning.

≈

Out of the 72,605 houses affected by the storm, 28,005 were completely destroyed. Ninety-five percent of the banana crop and 75 percent of the coffee crop were destroyed. Sixty-five percent of all poultry was gone. The entire electric system was shut down and 8 percent of the island lost telephone service. Roads were impassable due to the flooding and mudslides. The total damage was estimated at $3 billon, roughly $5.5 billion in 2023.

≈

Two people died from carbon monoxide poisoning. A family of four died after a candle set fire to their house while the mother was sleeping. One person died from head trauma after slipping and falling while removing water from his flooded home. An electrical company employee was electrocuted while repairing a damaged cable.

≈

"[…] Al día siguiente nos regresamos a nuestro hogar. Parecía otro país, no era el barrio Nuevo en el que me crié. Las casas de madera cerca de la de nosotros quedaron destrozadas, solo se podía ver el baño que era de cemento. La furia del huracán arrancó la mayoría de los árboles y ahora podía ver estructuras que quedaban a lo lejos de mi hogar que antes no podía ver; nada era igual.

Pasaron los días, no había luz, no había agua.

Ahí supe lo que vivieron nuestros abuelos cuando tenían que lavar ropa en los ríos. También tuve que ir a buscar agua en la quebrada para bajar los baños y hasta me bañé por primera vez en ese cuerpo de agua."

"On the next day we returned home. It looked like another country, it wasn't the Barrio Nuevo where I was raised. The wooden houses around us ended up destroyed; you could only see the bathrooms, which were made out of cement. The fury of the hurricane uprooted most of the trees and I could see the structures far away from my home that I hadn't been able to see before; nothing was the same.

The days passed: no light, no water.

That's when I knew how our grandparents lived when they had to wash clothes in the rivers. I also had to get water from the creek to flush the toilets, and I even bathed myself in that body of water for the first time."

—Luis Alfonso Oliveras Quiles, remembering Hurricane Georges in an op-ed for *Primera Hora*, September 21, 2022

Emergency Backpacks

I've had some version of these since I was a child, either under my bed or in a closet. I don't feel safe unless I know that at any point, I could pick up and leave my house. That I could run if I had to. A good emergency backpack contains enough to keep you alive for up to three days.

I've only had to actually run for my life once before, in my early twenties, from an electrical fire in the house I was renting.

Being acutely aware that everything can change in a second has mostly paid off in other ways. I can, for example, pack for a vacation in five minutes. I can move to a new city with two suitcases and a box. I can identify what is essential and put whatever that is in a neat, portable container.

This practice started around the time I was able to fully grasp the severity of natural disasters, between the ages of 10 and 14, which coincided with the time my mother got sick.

$$\approx$$

For the worst-case scenario, pack this:

Category	Items
Food	1. 10 granola bars (assorted) 2. 1 bag of trail mix and/or dried fruit 3. 1 full 27 oz. bottle of water 4. 1 bottle of water purifying tablets

Toiletries	1. Wet wipes 2. Tampons/pads/menstrual cup 3. Toothbrush 4. Floss 5. Extra medication
Underwear	1. 5 underpants (at most) 2. 3 pairs of socks
Pants	1. 1 pair of jeans 2. 1 pair of sweatpants
Shoes	1. 1 pair of sneakers, if possible (leave the house in boots or high-tops)
Shirts	1. 2 t-shirts, in addition to what you're wearing
Misc and Docs	1. Phone or tablet 2. Swiss Army knife, if available 3. 1 portable phone charger, if available 4. 1 headlamp and extra batteries 5. Passport 6. Social Security Card 7. Birth Certificate 8. Cash and wallet 9. 1 or 2 loved things

Ketchup and Mayonnaise

The day after Hurricane Georges, my mother was in good spirits. I grabbed my backpack and Cabbage Patch doll and we drove around to assess the wreckage. It was rare for us to go anywhere together just because, when there weren't drinks or parties or errands or other people awaiting her. This drive was special. There was no work to be done, indefinitely. No school for days, probably weeks. No electricity (the generator was only on at night). Just the two of us driving very slowly, down and around flooded streets and fallen trees. In our neighborhood in Guaynabo, most houses were built out of cement, so downed powerlines, trees, and mailboxes were the biggest threat to our neighborhood, in addition to flooding and broken windows.

≈

Hurricane season meant a lot of McDonald's and to-go meals, not that that wasn't the case for the rest of the year. As a 10-year-old, I didn't mind it, either. My mother didn't cook. Sometimes she would microwave chicken and potatoes. Once she made lasagna. There was another time she tried to bake a tray of brownies. We ate them burnt. The day after Georges we drove to Beba's to see if she had any food, but she and Buelo were making do with a portable gas stove, and we didn't want to overload her. So we went to the aptly named Bebo's Café—back then it was just one room—which was miraculously open, and ate chicharrones de pollo and tostones with mayoketchup (a mix of ketchup and mayonnaise). We then picked up my great-aunt and godmother Dahlia and her yippy dog, who'd been stuck in her apartment building all night, and waved at merengue singer Toño Rosario, who was having a few beers with friends on the hood of a car in the complex's parking lot.

≈

At home, the three of us had Pepsi with ice we bought at the pharmacy. Dahlia got out a handle of rum from the cabinet. The women drank and talked about men. I listened, always fascinated by the world of men and women, by the fact that my mother dated men, even though I had rarely seen her with one who wasn't a family member or a rando at a bar (though this would change before the end of the year). We played Operation and Monopoly by candlelight, sitting on the living room floor with the front door open to let the breeze in. We eventually all went to sleep in my tiny room, the one with the AC we would use when the generator was on.

Damage to homes in Toa Baja, Puerto Rico, on October 1, 1998, about a week after Hurricane Georges.

Passenger Seat

She was drunk often. She didn't have many friends. Her happiness was too exuberant, and so were her moments of despair, paralyzing even. Her few romantic relationships imploded.

≈

I was eight when I began to realize something was wrong. It was Christmas. We had gone to a party at a cousin's with my grandparents. My grandfather got sick on the patio after I spent half an hour asking him questions to keep him awake. *What's your favorite color? How are you? When was the last time you went to the movies?* Inside the house my mother fought with someone about driving drunk. I knew from past experience that she was going to drive drunk no matter what. And she did. Beba and I didn't know how to drive, not that it would've made a difference. She went against traffic on the wrong side of the expressway. Cars swerving around us at 75, 80 miles an hour. No amount of crying or screaming was going to prevent whatever was going to happen from happening. I knew then that we could've all died, just like she and I could've died a couple of months before if she had driven into that lamppost any faster.

≈

My mother's best friend stopped talking to her around 1998. I was 10. Her son had just had his first child, so she invited a few close friends to meet the baby. My mother's laugh woke me up from the nap I was taking in one of the rooms in their home. When I opened the door to see what was so funny, I saw my mother fall off her stool and flat on her back. I'd see her fall flat on her face on concrete on my 16th birthday, too. And a couple of other times. But this first time there was a group of women trying to shield me, telling me to go back to sleep. I locked myself in the bathroom instead, peeking through the air vents on the door to make sure she was still breathing. She passed out. After a couple of hours, she woke up and declared herself ready to drive us home, which was not true. The friend's son, the new father, took me into the baby's nursery. As he, a stranger, told me to be strong, I focused on the baby's whorl of hair. My mother opened the door of the nursery, a redheaded ghost. She grabbed my arm and said we were leaving. Her best friend, who'd come in right after, refused to let her take me, and I held onto the friend until my mother let me go. She looked at me like I had betrayed her, like I was rejecting everything she was, and I guess that was the first time I did. The next morning, my mother showed up hungover to take me home, and on the way she told me about how hurt she was, about how she had been fine, she had been totally fine. She never saw her friend again.

≈

I had this recurring nightmare almost every month in my mid-to-late twenties. I'm trying to drive a car from the passenger seat and lose control of the wheel. I always know when I'm about to crash, and I do.

Plantation Shutters

When I was 10, my mother's new boyfriend gave me a blue lovebird. I had never asked for one. I was scared of all animals. But I liked having something to name. I named him Kikirikí because he sounded like it. The cage he came in had no toys or perches. It sat on the kitchen counter, between the sink and a window with built-in black shutters. They're called plantation shutters, and they were the only kind we had in the house. They were rarely opened, except on cleaning days, when my mother would get down on her hands and knees and spot clean the entire floor with wet paper towels. She didn't like mopping.

I wouldn't touch the bird, just approached his cage every day after my morning pee to say hello. He pecked at my mother when she changed his water dish. A week after he got there, the cage was empty. My mother said he flew away. *He was sad you didn't play with him*, she said. It was so dark in our house, I hadn't realized how much better it was outside for a bird. The shutters had been closed the whole time.

Nightlight

A week after my mother was discharged from San Juan Capestrano—having recovered from the first of three episodes she had that year, each requiring 3- to 4-week-long hospitalizations—she opened my bedroom door in her underwear. She was crying, begging me not to leave. I was a young teenager; I couldn't go anywhere at 3:00 a.m. in a town with no public transportation.

In the days leading up to her committal, she'd call me at Beba's from her job at the Hospital Industrial and update me on the status of her memoir, which was nothing but notebooks full of chicken scratch piling up in the bathroom. She violently refused to use a computer. She'd cry out to her boyfriend when he was nowhere in sight. She'd drag me out of my grandmother's house after a bender, ignoring my pleas to let me stay. And then one day after work, she sat in my grandparents' rocking chair and stopped speaking. She rocked herself and stared at the wall and smiled blankly, like the star of a Lifetime movie tackling mental illness very badly. It didn't matter how hard I cried or how long I screamed or how close to her face I got. She wasn't there. It was like seeing the devil come.

≈

I'm not sure why or how I went back to living with her so soon after she got out of the hospital, but there I was, very afraid for my mother and for myself and with nowhere to go. After she went back to sleep, I stared at my night-light and prayed faithfully for the first time in my life.

≈

My mother had met Johnny in high school, but didn't pay attention to him until their 20th high school reunion. He was a short, quiet chemist with two sons from a previous marriage that had ended amicably. By then, I was used to her being with men who yelled or stole her credit cards, so even though I hated being dragged out to so many of their dates, a part of me was relieved that she had found someone sweet. I remember the gaudy fish vase he sent to Beba's for when she got back from the hospital, and the calm way he spelled out for me what bipolar disorder and psychotic episodes were. Eventually, the time between calls grew longer, a type of gradual coldness that I've become familiar with in my own romantic life, until the calls stopped altogether after she was discharged for the third time that year.

≈

Her face was covered in boils. It must've been the drug cocktails, the lack of baths, or a combination of the two. My mother struggled with acne her whole life, as have I, and had a strict cleaning and medication routine for many years that had kept it under control. But when I saw her again, she was a raw nerve. The very core of who she was, the pain, imbalance, and fear, were all showing on her body. She had lost close to 30 pounds. My grandmother, at a loss for real solutions, spent the week before her return buying her pajama sets. Dozens of them. Cute, cheap cotton ones in different pastel colors, with tiny flowers and geometric shapes, the kind I used to wear to sleep when I was little.

≈

It's hard to describe the feeling of losing a live parent. Neither of mine have died. I must have looked at her the way she looked at me when I ran into her estranged friend's arms instead of hers. It's not that I had been safe before, but it was obvious now that I'd never be safe. I saw how fast a person could disappear.

Bright Eyes

While my mother was in outpatient therapy a year later, my father took me to live with him. I was there between the ages of 15 and 17. At first, I was mostly relieved to be in a place close to my baby half-sister and stepbrother, with a computer and a certain sense of normalcy. At first, I was only meant to be there for a few weeks, but my mother kept getting sick.

≈

I changed friend groups to fit my new bad attitude. I wasted hours downloading Bright Eyes songs. I updated my LiveJournal with cryptic quotes directed at boys who wronged me. I had my first kiss. I went to punk shows. I got drunk for the first time. I did coke for the first time. I hung out with girls who humiliated me for fun. I learned to drive. I was roughed up, felt up. I played tragic whores in school plays. I got a job at the local Ben & Jerry's. I backpacked alone. I got a high school scholarship. I spoke back to my father. I chopped off all my hair.

≈

My father told me about the women he bedded—how this woman cried when they made love, how that other one sent him nudes. I had to go back home with him, to my baby sister and brother, to their mother, and keep those secrets, which burned in me like bile. I don't know why he chose to tell me, his teenage daughter, while I was trying to become myself, while my own mother wasted away. Other things happened, but this is probably good for now.

Socks in the Mail

I was one of the 525,769 Puerto Ricans who moved to the United States between 2006 (when I graduated from high school) and 2016. I was part of the reason the island lost 14 percent of its population during that time. I had done fairly well in school and assumed I'd get a scholarship to some liberal arts college in the northeastern United States, like people who liked the things I liked did in the movies. NYC was where romantics went, and I had been romantic about the city since I watched a VH1 documentary on the year 1977. My English was good enough.

So I got the scholarship, opened my first bank account, and moved to the West Village, into a dorm that was prohibitively expensive. I only stayed there a year before moving into a curtained-off living room with two other girls in a shared East Village apartment. I took out loans, did the work-study thing, got a few gigs here and there. I had brought everything I owned in two suitcases. I didn't have a coat, just layers of jackets my stepmother gave me before I left. My mother, who went back to work at the hospital halfway through my senior year of high school, would mail me a check for a hundred dollars every month, for food and books. She would also mail socks and pens. My father, who was out of a steady job, sent me a couple hundred from time to time, too. I later found out my stepmother made those transfers, including anything else I needed to make rent on difficult months, from her account.

One of my cousins had also gone to the States for school, so it didn't come as a shock to Beba and Buelo that I would want to leave. They said there was nothing for me back home in terms of job security or prospects. So did my mother. And at the time it really did seem that way. My parents would have preferred it if I'd stayed on the island for university and left after I'd lived on my own, but near them, for a while. But I couldn't bear being near them anymore. I wanted anything else. I wanted to contrive a romantic me into being, disassociate in as many ways as my work-study money could afford.

Look Who It Is

When the excitement of moving away wore off, I became hyperaware of my inadequacy. There was the constant fear of the floor giving into the weight of who I wasn't. I had seen terrible things before I turned 18, but I didn't know about credit, or sexual health, or how to be part of a group or form healthy bonds. It took me six months to get on the subway. I was afraid of public transportation, of being seen by thousands of people, of showing strangers how ill-equipped I was to ride the train and live my life. I walked around with MapQuest printouts and drank 40s to feel like I could join in whatever fun people were having around me.

For the first couple years, I couldn't wait to go home again to the people and things that felt normal to me, but memories from my childhood and destructive coping mechanisms took over, and my grasp on the island and my family slipped. I don't remember much of my early twenties, other than most of those years were spent acting out scenes I'd seen before, over and over again. I know I put myself in dangerous situations. I know my English lost its slight accent. There were a couple of pregnancy scares, some health issues. Some sexual violence. There was too much alcohol. There was disciplinary probation (after I got caught smoking in the tub; they didn't see the coke). Parties in lofts. The calls home trickled to weekly check-ins filled with lies.

Buelo died of pneumonia during my third year away. I last saw him at the veterans hospital in Río Piedras a couple of months before. He looked like a belly-up spider, an ancient, shriveled baby. Tubes and IVs protruded from every orifice and limb. He could probably tell I was afraid. *Mira quien es*, he said. *Look who it is*. He smiled for a second and didn't say much else. Beba kept busy as she always did, talking about things she could still control and rearranging the room when she wasn't crying.

I was asked to write a eulogy, which my father, who always loved Buelo, read on my behalf. I didn't go to the funeral, and I don't remember why. Buelo gave my life a historical authenticity, I wrote; he was my connection to a place that was "running away from me." I don't know what that means. But it's true that after he died, my active attachment to the island weakened. He had been like a father to me after all.

I got it together enough to intern at a journal and graduate a semester early. I wrote for the college newspaper and had a lovely boyfriend who didn't know what he had signed up for. News about where the island was headed was grim. And it wasn't uncommon for my father or mother to tell me that I did good by leaving. I became synonymous with leaving. My mother got sick again, but it was easy for Beba to hide the worst parts when we talked. My father was as financially unstable as ever.

V. Hurricane Sandy

Satellite image of Hurricane Sandy over northeastern United States on October 29, 2012.

Historical Notes

In 2006, Congress officially ended the special tax breaks that had incentivized U.S. corporations to bring work to the island and helped boost the Puerto Rican economy since 1976. This came 10 years after President Bill Clinton signed the Small Business Job Protection Act, which increased the federal hourly minimum wage from $4.25 to $5.15, into law. Around the same time, he signed legislation that phased out section 936, which granted the aforementioned tax breaks, in order to offset the federal revenue losses that came with those and also help pay for the minimum-wage raise.

The island's job market has been suffering ever since.

≈

During the 10-year phase-out period of the federal tax code, companies that had benefited from the latter moved their businesses out of the island, leaving not only fewer jobs for people, but also tax shortfalls that led the government to over-borrow and issue bonds frenetically.

≈

Financial institutions such as Santander Bank, Morgan Stanley, and Citigroup capitalized on the crisis during this 10-year period by continuing to extend credit even after it was clear that the island would not be able to pay the money back.

≈

Puerto Rico has lost more than 20 percent of its jobs since 2007. In 2021, the unemployment rate was 8.7 percent.

≈

In 2012, the number of Puerto Ricans (and their U.S.-born descendants) in the 50 states of the U.S. reached 4.9 million. Out of those, around 730,000 lived in NYC, and close to 448,000 lived in New Jersey. That same year, there were 3.6 million Puerto Ricans living on the island.

≈

On November 8, 2012, Puerto Ricans on the island (61 percent of them) supported U.S. statehood in a non-binding referendum for the first time.

By 2017, there were 5.6 million Puerto Ricans in the U.S. and 3.3 million on the island.

Beba

Princeton
October 28, 2012

A stone pushes down on my chest
when I look out at the cemetery, at the storm
throwing plastic bottles, turtle shell combs,
against the tombstones of people
I don't know.

I look out at the graves of Grover Cleveland
and Samuel Davies,
foreign and white and buried,
more present to me in death than when you were
alive, weeks ago.

The stone in my chest is tomb gray.
So was your face when I last saw you
and bathed you like you bathed me
on the day I was born.

I am not a good daughter.
You always said so, before.
Now the dead run for cover down the street.

My mother called in the morning
and you were gone.
It hasn't stopped raining since.

Hurricane Sandy

On its way to the U.S. from the Bahamas, Hurricane Sandy downgraded to a Category 1, with winds of up to 80 mph. On October 27, it downgraded to tropical storm, only to regain power and upgrade to a Category 1 again. By the time it made landfall in the U.S., on October 29, it was a Category 2 with hurricane force winds that extended 175 miles from the eye of the storm.

≈

According to the National Hurricane Center, Sandy caused at least 147 deaths in the U.S., Canada, and the Caribbean. Forty-eight of them were in New York, where coastal neighborhoods like Breezy Point in the Rockaways are still recovering over 10 years later. Fifty-four deaths were reported in Haiti.

≈

The storm caused $70 billion worth of damage. 8.5 million people lost power. The East and Hudson rivers overflowed into Manhattan, flooding subway platforms and tunnels. Coastal New Jersey was badly hit—a huge section of the Atlantic City boardwalk was destroyed, as well as businesses and homes. There was a full moon on October 29, which strengthened the storm surge.

≈

Puerto Rico was mostly spared by Hurricane Sandy. The only known casualty was a man in his fifties, from the southern town of Juana Díaz, who drowned trying to cross a flooded river.

Bubba Gump

I had been perfecting self-sabotaging patterns for a few years, but this came to a head shortly after graduating from college, during my first semester at journalism school. On the surface, things were fine. I lived in a nice Queens apartment with two other women. My college boyfriend was right down the street and attending the same program. At college graduation, my mother and father had been in the same room together, for me, for the first time in many years, and neither one killed the other. I was 22, in a relationship, in a great program. Friends and family rooted for me.

Then, after a particularly taxing day chasing stories, my boyfriend and I were sitting in the Bubba Gump Shrimp in Times Square of all places, and I decided, just like that, that I'd quit school. I had been getting blackout drunk regularly, picking fights with the only man who could stand me, lying to him, and forcing myself to pursue a career my father had deemed appropriate for me, while getting deeper into debt and not really writing what I wanted to. What I wanted to write, I didn't know.

≈

Like many people in their early twenties who have time to examine their feelings, I was confused and afraid. I didn't want my life, which was a relatively easy one on the outside, considering the Recession. Getting out of bed was difficult. I was an impostor. I was forgetting my Spanish. My English didn't feel organic. I didn't know where home was. I didn't care about anything, really. I called my mother first. She was a passive observer. Disappointed, but cushioned by medication. Then I called my father, and the next day I completely regretted it. But it was too late.

≈

There had been no reason to explain my decision to my parents. But I needed to justify my existing here, my taking up space and changing my mind, to someone. The only job I was able to find was as a receptionist at a dojo. Andrew McCarthy's son went there. Then I got an internship at a literary agency that paid in lunch, then a job as a buyer at a bookstore, then a job in Princeton, in the copyright office of the university's press. I left my boyfriend, someone I would've married when the time was right.

≈

From the time I was 22 on, I made lateral moves, alternating between low-paying positions in publishing and low-paying positions in service or retail. Whenever something felt semi-comfortable, I'd move into another apartment or another job in the name of the stability I was also running away from. There was time to write, but I chose to work on other people's words instead. It seemed more important to make money, and deal with myself and my writing later.

Carry-on Bag

The day I moved to Princeton, the house I was renting a room in caught fire. I had made the trek there from Queens, with my now ex-boyfriend and two goldfish, following a moving truck that cost me all of my savings.

≈

A move is always at least a little traumatic, but I was an expert by then. I unpacked everything that night and tried to make the room homey, despite the beige rug and wood paneling. Around 4:00 am, my housemate swung the bedroom door open and yelled at me to get out of the house right now. The only thing I could make out as she ran out of the room, in tears, was, *fire, first floor*. I got out of bed and put on my rubber boots, grabbed my laptop, and put it in a carry-on bag, along with half of the clothes that were hung in the closet. I knew from always keeping an emergency backpack to get two pairs of shoes, my passport, social security card, birth certificate, wallet, phone, laptop, charger, and a photo album. Not until I was standing in front of the burning building with the housemate, the landlady, her boyfriend, and the firefighters did I realize I was only wearing a robe and it was November.

≈

After the fire I lived in a motel for two months. I lost 30 pounds. I made friends with all the shuttle drivers who dropped me off at work and picked me up after. Then a coworker told me about a dingy duplex with a backyard that was up for rent in town. I shared it with an Olympic rower. She ate salad with her hands and was training to go to the 2012 Olympics in London. She ended up not making the team, and her mother flew in from Washington state to tend to her daughter, who was beyond distraught. They were devout

Christians and watched Disney movies that whole week. On my way out one day, the mother grabbed my arm and told me, *You do understand. I'm sorry I've been crowding you. But you look like someone who's been through some loss, so you understand.*

Ivy

During my time in Princeton, I kept drinking until I blacked out, slept around, got a cat. The coworker moved in that October. The rower moved out. I spent Hurricane Sandy alone in the duplex (the coworker was at a wedding in Massachusetts) with my friend Tim on the phone. He was in love with the coworker, which I resented.

≈

After my father started to tell me, over the phone, about the college student he'd been talking to, I interrupted him to remind him of the woman he had at home who loved him. He had just separated from his wife of 20 years and was living with someone new. I began the process of estrangement. He blamed my mother for putting thoughts in my head, my mother, whose main concern was finding stability and routine, preventing future episodes. He wasn't the person he told me—and told himself—he was.

≈

My stepmother and I remained friendly after the separation. We still talk sometimes, about jobs and boyfriends, mostly. I wasn't there for the end of their relationship, and I can't say that I expected it. But it didn't surprise me either.

≈

I got a therapist and saw her once a week, a privilege paid for by my job at the time. I had never openly talked to anyone about the truly bad things, the things I was ashamed of. About the time a man I trusted took me out drinking when his wife was away until I lost myself and woke up naked in his living room. About the time I asked a guy to stop, and he didn't. About how

I went to the movies with my mother the next day, despite the nausea. About how both of those things happened within the span of a month when I was 18 and home for the holidays on my first year away. About the time some other guy forced his hands up my skirt outside my apartment in Queens. About other occurrences. More than anything, it scared me to hear that these violations were not my fault. I was afraid of what that made them, and of what that made me.

≈

Shortly before Hurricane Sandy, on October 4, Beba died. My mother called me that morning. I was in a friend's bed. I told my boss the news and he let me take the day off. I took a bottle of wine home, drank it, and fell asleep until the sun rose the next day. I didn't go to the funeral.

An overflight shows some of the damage that Hurricane Sandy caused when it hit the New Jersey coast at the end of October 2012.

Sangría

On the way to the nursing home, my mother showed little emotion. I had flown down to PR for the weekend to visit Beba, whose cognitive health plummeted after Buelo died. My mother did her best to prepare me for what I was going to see, but she herself had lost a lot of language to the medication. She was still drinking, too.

I am not sure why my mother and Pablo chose that particular nursing home. I imagine it was because it was in Río Piedras, where she had always lived. A dilapidated daycare, something between a prison and a home, its walls were painted a vomit beige. It was hot. The sweet and acrid smell of soiled sheets and everyone's sweat hit you across the face as soon as you walked in. My grandmother sat alone in the TV room, staring into space, much like my mother did when in the middle of a psychotic episode. I sat next to her, but she wouldn't face me. My mother asked her if she knew who I was. *Providencia*, she said. I said my name. She repeated it.

My mother insisted that Beba wanted to have a sangria in Old San Juan and go for a drive along the coast. I never heard Beba say that, and it seemed irresponsible, but we went anyway. My mother and Pablo ordered drinks and croquettes, and Beba had no reaction when we begged her to eat. My mother put the drink to Beba's mouth and my grandmother drank to the best of her ability. She knew then to smile from time to time. It is engrained in us to smile. The smile and the eyes were infinitely apart. Her beautiful, moonlike face hung from her bones. Her fingernails were dirty. But the nurse had dressed her for a day out, a flowery matching set.

Beba pointed at the bathroom. She had been here before and knew where it was. My mother insisted I help change her diaper. Beba held onto the bars in the stall and stared at the wall as my mother took off the diaper and I tried to keep her from falling over. My mother left us there because she couldn't handle it. None of us could handle it. I don't know who this outing was for. I cleaned her up and dressed her, talked to her as if this was completely natural—she was like a mother to me anyway—as if she could feel shame. We walked back to the table and got the check.

≈

A couple of years ago, I dated a man who told me that on his cousin's farm in Ireland, he mistook a dove for a pigeon, and shot it dead. He had heard somewhere that doves mate for life, so he went out looking for its partner so it wouldn't have to wonder where the dead one went. He never found her.

≈

My mother and Pablo checked Beba back into the home. I stayed behind and cried in the car. That was the last time I saw her.

≈

When I was learning English as a child, I thought that mourning doves exclusively sang in the morning.

Wino/Forever

The one time I was truly lucky was like a lot of other times I was lucky, so the details don't really matter. The miracle was always waking up from a blackout, whether or not I wanted to. A hangover meant I was still alive. A floor meant I was under a roof. Being in possession of my wallet meant I could use the insurance card if I was hurt. Wandering blacked out, strangers at bars, flinging myself into hard surfaces if I felt especially bold—I brought most of these accidents on. It was like holding the door wide open for a deranged sister to come around and wreck my house. My mother had always driven us to church wacked out of her mind, so we had to keep things familiar. I only want to know the kind of luck that keeps you from being run over when you're not doing anything wrong, not the kind that catches you when you throw yourself off a cliff.

Pelúa

Hurricane Sandy was the first storm I remember spending alone. I remained isolated for a few days after, still numb from my grandmother's death, and without power. Where I was, in central New Jersey, cleanup and recovery were in no way comparable to what coastal New Jersey and the Rockaways endured and continued to go through for years to come. Even though PR was basically unscathed by the hurricane, I decided to spend that Christmas with my friend Tim and his family near the Jersey Shore. Their home was intact, but a few miles away a neighborhood had been completely eroded, stripped of boardwalks and people. Scattered unfinished and abandoned developments lined the shore, like time had stopped. Back in NYC, friends helped with hurricane relief in the Rockaways, rebuilt, and even started schools. I didn't offer to help, and mainly went about my life. I may have seemed like I could've done more than donate money, but taking care of myself took everything I had.

≈

By 2012, my mother and I were more like acquaintances who happened to talk to each other almost every day. Even now, 10 years later, we go through the same phone routine. If I don't answer the phone, she won't text. She'll just keep calling and leaving voicemails. They're all between seven and 10 seconds long and have the same content. The greeting is always, *Pelúa de mami, llámame cuando puedas.* The direct translation from the Spanish is something like, "Mom's little hairy one, call me when you can." The reason for the call is never spelled out.

≈

The word "pelúa" is an informal version of "peluda," meaning "hairy." While I am, indeed, a hairy woman, and this comes with its own set of socially imposed hang-ups, calling someone "pelúa" in Puerto Rico is most likely a sweet, if teasing, gesture. A bad situation can be deemed "pelúa," too, however.

≈

I didn't answer yesterday because I was getting a biopsy. Today, some time before I wrote this, I didn't answer because I spent a long time removing the bandage and putting a new one over my stitches, trying not to vomit. I called her back when I was done. She told me she had called me yesterday. *Why didn't you answer me?* I said, *I was getting a biopsy, remember.* She said, *But I called you.* I said, *I was having surgery!* She said, *Don't talk to me like that, I am very sensitive right now.* She was on her way to a routine mammogram. Her hips were hurting. She was going to Chili's tonight. She said, *I love you very much.* I say, *Me too*, every time, because I don't want to talk about it.

VI. Hurricane María

Satellite image of Hurricane María over Puerto Rico, completely covering the island on September 20, 2017.

Historical Notes

Adding to the economic crisis in Puerto Rico was and is the mismanagement of public funds, the privatization of infrastructure as basic as the electrical grid, and corruption preceding and related to the phase out of tax incentives. This, along with insufficient federal social funding, has led to a mass exodus of residents.

≈

Puerto Rico receives $373 million in federal funding a year for Medicaid, which more than half of Puerto Ricans use, while individual states receive billions. In 2020, Medicaid expenditures in Puerto Rico were projected to reach $2.8 billion.

≈

The debt crisis has caused insurance companies to delay doctors' paychecks and influence medical decisions that ultimately affect the quality of treatment plans. Seven hundred doctors left the island in 2016 alone.

≈

Puerto Rico receives 55 cents for every dollar it spent on Medicaid. Mississippi received almost 76 cents in 2021, even though the poverty rate in PR (almost 44 percent in 2022) is far higher than in Mississippi (almost 19 percent in 2022), the poorest state in the United States.

≈

In 2014, the U.S. Census Bureau reported that the island's total population went down from 3.7 million in 2010 to 3.6 million in 2013. In 2020, there were approximately 3.3 million Puerto Ricans on the island. Between 2010 and 2020, PR lost 11.8 percent of its people.

≈

Puerto Rico has the highest possible general sales tax in America: 11.5 percent.

≈

In May of 2017, Puerto Rico owed $74 billion in debts and more than $53 billion in unfunded pensions. Teachers and government workers might not be able to retire.

≈

In 2016, the U.S. Congress formed the Financial Oversight and Management Board for Puerto Rico, known on the island as La Junta. They have authority over the island's budget and were meant to revise and approve budget and spending. In early 2022, a restructuring bill was put in place to reduce around $33 billion in debt to $7.4 billion. The deal is also meant to "save" the government more than $50 billion in debt payments.

The bankruptcies of other public entities, including the Puerto Rico Electric Power Authority (PREPA), which filed for it just two months before María hit, remain unresolved at the time of writing. A private U.S.-Canadian company, LUMA, was hired by La Junta as part of the fiscal plan to take over the distribution and transmission of the power grid of the island— further devastated by recent earthquakes and hurricanes—from PREPA in the summer of 2021. This privatization of the electrical grid and the ensuing hikes to electricity bills (seven increases in one year, to be exact), will be used to pay bondholders. Since LUMA took over, blackouts are a common occurrence, leaving homes, hospitals, and schools without power. La Junta can nullify laws brought forth by the island's legislature if they are incompatible with their debt adjustment plan.

In 2022, Puerto Rico's Governor, Pedro Pierluisi, vetoed Bill PC 1383, which would have protected PREPA workers' retirement benefits and pensions from being diverted to pay for the public debt. 18,000 families depended on those pensions.

I, II

Two months after the storm
a PR doctor spoke to the *Times*
about the new definition
of okay.
"It's I survived.
My family
didn't die."

What family
do I have?
I ask myself
from the "mainland"
from the light shining
on a workshop table,
from a tank full of gas,
a working kitchen.

So I call you, Mom,
at your house,
my old house,
a sailboat
sinking
surely

into the ground
(volcanic rock is
perfidious
at best).

I want to know if
"What we have lost
is the foundation
that holds a society
together,"
like the doctor said.

But you're not there,
but neither am I,
and there is no cord or line
to get through,
no way of knowing anything
at all,
which is what I'd wanted
before there was more to leave,
before there was more to say than,
"I survived
and my family didn't die,"

did it?

Hurricane María

Hurricane María originated as a tropical wave on the western coast of Africa, making its way across the Atlantic Ocean between September 10 and September 16, 2017. On September 16, 700 miles southeast of the Lesser Antilles, it intensified into a tropical depression. Within hours, it was a tropical storm with maximum sustained winds of 50 mph. By September 17, it had become the eighth hurricane of the season, with maximum sustained winds of 75 mph. By the time it made landfall in Dominica on September 19, it was a Category 5 hurricane. The following morning, on September 20, Hurricane María made landfall in Yabucoa, southeastern Puerto Rico, as a Category 4 hurricane with winds of 155 mph. It weakened slightly as it made its way through the island only to regain some strength near the Dominican Republic, Haiti, and the Bahamas. Moving north and away from the United States made the hurricane weaken quickly, until it dissipated by the end of September.

≈

In Puerto Rico, entire coastal neighborhoods like La Perla in Old San Juan were destroyed. People in some areas saw six feet of water, some up to 15, flood their homes. Eighteen million coffee trees were pulled out of the ground. Nearly all residents lost power. Some didn't have power again for an entire year. In the weeks following the storm, families in the mountains buried their dead in backyards, people raided corner stores for any canned foods they could find, shared generators, parked their cars on the highway and prayed for service so they could tell anyone they could reach that they were alive and safe for now.

≈

María is the feminine variant of the Roman name Marius. It also derives from the Latin word *mare*, meaning "sea."

≈

The 10th most intense Atlantic hurricane on record, and the worst one Puerto Rico had endured since San Felipe Segundo in 1928, María cost more than $100 million (2022 USD) in damages.

≈

In May of 2018, a study published by *The New England Journal of Medicine* estimated that roughly 4,600 deaths were caused by Hurricane María, many of them due to delayed medical care or lack of access to it. The official tally in December 2017 had been 64. The government of Puerto Rico admitted in August 2018 that the number may be greater than 64.

≈

According to the Census Bureau, 129,848 people left the island between July 2017 and July 2018. That is roughly 4 percent of the Puerto Rican population.

≈

Thirteen days after the hurricane, President Donald J. Trump visited the island for the first time since the disaster. He threw paper towels into a crowd at a Guaynabo chapel. *Great people*, he said.

≈

Despite the fact that FEMA had been anticipating for years that "the territory would require extensive federal support in moving commodities" after a natural disaster, the island received only $6 million within the first nine days after the hurricane's landfall, unlike Hurricane Harvey survivors in Texas, who received $100 million from the agency during the same period despite the greater threat to human life and infrastructure in post-María PR. FEMA listed supply and staff shortages, poor communication, and shipment mislabeling as factors that led to the government's gross negligence. "An incredible unsung success," Trump later called the response.

Trenton Makes, the World Takes

During my time in New Jersey, my body wasn't mine. I saw it from above, going through people and tasks as if doing so would fill the void of home. The shape of that void, however, shifted daily. Near what I didn't yet know was the end of my stay in Princeton, I answered a Craigslist Missed Connections ad. He lived 45 minutes away, in Philadelphia. We emailed for a month before deciding to meet. The train I took to see him ran parallel to a bridge with a large sign that read, "Trenton Makes, the World Takes," like a mother guilt tripping her children.

≈

The man who wrote the ad was leaning against a wall outside of the Standard Tap, with his hands in his jacket pockets and a leg folded under him like a sweet, longhaired flamingo. He had been taller and less delicate in my mind. He was looking for my floating head like a person wondering where the waiter was with his food. Had I known that he'd always be hungry, that he had someone at home already, I would've taken the first train back to Jersey. I walked up to him with my guts in a knot, overwhelmed by the fact that someone would wait for me in the cold when there was a fire inside.

≈

Even after I found out he cheated, I continued our long-distance relationship. I quit my job and moved back to New York because I missed my friends, and I missed feeling justified in my stagnancy. Still I continued to see him. I loved this man, and maybe he loved me. But neither of us knew how to be still or truthful. He hurt me, so I punished him as best as I could, with words, with emotional outbursts, with self-destruction. Dying for him was almost a full-time job. When at last he disappeared, because one of us had to, I saw how messed up everything was.

≈

If I was a house, I was a crumbling one, gothic-style, with a woman in the attic waiting to set fire to it all. I had taken vacations from this house here and there: I'd leave and have fun, stick to anyone who wanted me, force romantic relationships on people I'd known for weeks and friendships with incompatible women, desperately. But that uneven pile of rocks was what I had to return to.

Peau d'Orange

When I moved back to New York, hardly any of my friends remained. People had married, stopped drinking, moved away, had children. For two years I sat in medicated stupor at a desk in midtown Manhattan, filling hundreds of Excel spreadsheets with the names and emails of biology professors who used the textbooks my company edited. Management called this "market research," something I was told was essential in keeping the wheels turning. Chipping away at—gnawing on—sitting on—dingbats—phrases otherwise ignoble were all part of the lulling language my coworkers used to make and talk about business. I'd take more medicine than I should have to pass the day, to soften my feelings toward the repetitive work and the daily realization that life was no better outside of that office.

≈

The drinking and the pills and the not eating gave me shingles. I fainted on the subway. I lay in bed for days at a time, only breaking to pee or get a handful of nuts or water. No one but my mother called. Every once in a while, I'd put on something attractive and go to a bar and pretend to read a book, only to go home alone after making out with a stranger at four in the morning. Then I'd wake up at six to go to work, to the immunology glossaries, the T-cell counts, the peau d'orange. I had worked my way up from filling out Excel spreadsheets to spending months staring at tumors, asking doctors for pictures of their patients' diseased breasts and lungs, and calling them again to ask for better resolution. Skin and lungs, ovaries, organs that no longer belonged to people, that I examined in a haze for printers, so that medical students could pay money to study from them. I would talk to oncologists, neurologists, men and women who carried the weight of other people's lives quite literally every day, and who, despite the pressure and the constant death, had a sense of humor and argued with me about font choices for their chapter headings.

≈

I did well enough at work to not arouse suspicion, despite all the damage I had been doing to my body and brain. No one knew that the personal emergency I had to tend to when I took a couple of weeks off at the last minute was that I could barely get out of my closet after a particularly bad bender. I looked completely fine, relaxed even, in front of coworkers and authors. But outside of the office, I couldn't really hold a conversation, and sober social situations made me panic. I was ill, and the medicine I chose was only making me sicker.

Passionflower

I managed to apply to graduate school again, and somehow got a full ride. I wanted to finish what I started five years before. School was on Long Island, by the ocean. I wanted to be close to water. I needed to quit pills. And I didn't want to wait an entire summer for the semester to start before leaving the city. So I put my few things in storage and went to work for a retired chiropractor and his family on a farm in the Kennebec Highlands in exchange for room and board. I found them on the World Wide Organization of Organic Farms website.

≈

My bunkmate was a doula from Brooklyn who taught me how to read tarot and use passionflower tinctures. Every morning, before getting out of bed, she would record her dreams in a notebook she kept under the pillow. If she couldn't remember her dreams, she would free write for 10 minutes. I called myself a writer in private but didn't have a daily practice like she did.

≈

Her father would mail her *The New York Times* crossword puzzle, and soon he began sending me his regards and extra puzzles. I had no contact with my father, hadn't for years. My mother thought what I was doing, for free, was odd. And it was. Generations of men and women in my family fought to dig themselves out from arrangements like this. My great-uncle worked in a quarry so Buelo could go to university. There was, undoubtedly, a lack of respect in my turning manual labor into rehab.

≈

The doula and I became our sources of comfort on the farm, which was run like a factory. We shared the work, put on the stilts (to harvest tomatoes at the top of the vines) when the other was tired, washed the lettuce while the other sorted, drove to town and snuck contraband chips and sheet masks into the house. Sometimes we'd grab a margarita from the only Mexican place in town and smoke a cigarette on the way back.

≈

We were 30, but I felt 13. My skin browned. Dark freckles appeared on my nose after hundreds of hours pushing wheelbarrows full of dirt uphill, uprooting entire beds of snap peas, and weeding fields full of milkweed and crabgrass by hand. No one there knew the reason behind the dizziness, the breakouts all over my body, the mood swings, the nausea. They could all chalk it up to the sun constantly beating us down. It was also easier to hide that I was detoxing because everyone had jobs to do. I gradually got better. I got stronger. I was healthier, in more ways than anyone could know.

Six of Swords

There was nothing to do after dark on the farm. We would talk after dinner or swim in the lake and then go to our respective beds, letting the whir of the fan and the wind and the crickets outside sing us to sleep. My dreams became more vivid, and I could insert myself and change their outcomes. I recognized the scenes. Me in a car, trying to drive from the passenger seat, knowing I would crash. One night, I called out, as if I were the director of the movie. Stop the car. Stop it right now. And it did. After that, it was all water, dreams of being dragged by big, vertiginous waves, of giant, shiny gray sea mammals jumping in and out of indoor swimming pools, of pink lagoons behind glass, bioluminescent shrimp. I'd wake up and record these in detail, get at them slowly, as if they were the only piece of food I'd have that day.

≈

Almost every other day, I'd draw the Six of Swords by chance, a card in the minor arcana depicting a journey over water. A man rows a boat carrying a cloaked person and six swords. We can't see their faces, but we can see the shore they're moving toward. The divinatory meaning has something to do with missions and the silence after a storm.

Mancha de Plátano /Plantain Stain

On the farm I learned that every egg starts off white. Calcium carbonate, the stuff from crushed oyster shells in chicken feed that also makes paper white, is the reason. Whatever happens inside the mother determines the egg's final pigment, in the same way we carry our mothers' pain.

≈

A white egg turns brown when it's laid by a Rhode Island Red or an Australorps or a Welsummer or any other brown-gened lady. The break-down of red blood cells produces something called *protoporphyrin* that stains it. The white on the inside is preserved.

≈

A white egg turns blue when an Araucana or an Ameraucana or a Cream Legbar starts laying. Blue starts in the bile, infusing the inside and outside of the shell. The blue pigment is called *oocyanin,* like "ocean," "cyan."

≈

A white egg turns green when a chocolate brown-laying breed is crossed with a blue-biled Ameraucana. The blue seeps through at the beginning of the journey down the oviduct, and can still be seen through the brown, making it a soft olive green.

≈

The more intense the pigment, the higher the quality of the female.

Our Walking Life

In my sleep
I drive from the passenger seat.
In my waking life
my mother drooled at the wheel;
my fingers were too small
to wrap themselves around it.

I'll dream of stray dogs
hanging from my arms by their teeth.
In my walking life
the ceiling beams fell on our heads
and my bones were too soft to run
when I should have.

All the murky water of some other night
will be there in place of every inscrutable person
I held in love.

An octopus's ink will sludge down my throat.
In my talking life
at the foot of my bed with an old quote
my father brushed off
what I saw in the dark.

He said with his big hands,
for all life is a dream
and dreams themselves are only dreams.
But if that were true, he would've sat
and listened.

Noyac Road

I settled into my new home on Long Island a couple of weeks before Hurricane María made landfall in Puerto Rico. Blindly emailing people from my cohort at school, I had found two women who were willing to split the rent for a place near the campus. Houses in some parts of the Hamptons are vacant between Labor Day and Memorial Day, a window of time that conveniently coincides with the school year. It's also what rich Hamptonites consider winter, hence renting out their properties for cheap(er) during those eight months.

≈

The house we rented was still too expensive. To get to it, you had to drive down Noyac Road, bordered by dogwood trees and paths that led to grand, empty manors. There was a fire pit, a shed, a trampoline and treehouse where the landlord's children used to play, a canoe, hydrangeas, wisteria, Japanese maples, and a deck. A 15-minute walk to Towd Point Beach. The landlord could tell we were trying to control our excitement, so he upped the rent and we signed.

≈

Our school was on Shinnecock Nation land, on the south shore of eastern Long Island, in and around what is now Southampton. The name "Shinnecock" means something like "people of the stony shore" in Algonquian. Beba and Buelo's house was in Río Piedras, Rock River. I wanted to believe that that synchronicity meant I was on the right path.

≈

Before European colonizers arrived in the 1600s, Shinnecock territory stretched from Mastic to East Hampton, roughly 36 miles. By 1859, the

Shinnecock reservation was reduced to 3.2 km², which hasn't changed despite land claims filed against New York State by tribal members. It is a 15-minute drive from the $145-million dollar Jule Pond estate, built for Henry Ford, of Ford Motors fame. Henry Ford once said, "History is more or less bunk."

≈

On one of our first days in town, the housemates and I went to the annual Shinnecock powwow. A charter school bus picked us up near their outpost on Montauk Highway. We gathered under a cloud of smoke and ate 12-dollar tacos made with pita bread and Hormel chili next to other people who didn't dare to comment on the price. The woman who held my taco out for me folded it inside a napkin. She didn't look me in the eye. There was a Taíno booth selling reproductions of cemíes nearby. My housemates took a picture of me by it. *Look, your people,* one of them said. A facsimile of a facsimile of a facsimile.

Earlier that day, in Southampton Village, by a Citarella, we posed for a photograph in front of a sign that read, "NOTICE: ALL PERSONS ARE REQUIRED TO WEAR PROPER ATTIRE ON OUR PUBLIC STREETS Inc. Village of Southampton Ord. #82."

"Far as the human eye could see,
　　　　Were stretched the fields of waving corn.
Soft on my ear the warbling birds
　　　　Were heralding the birth of morn.
While here and there a cottage quaint
　　　　Seemed to repose in quiet ease
Amid the trees, whose leaflets waved
　　　　And fluttered in the passing breeze.
O morning hour! so dear thy joy,
　　　　And how I longed for thee to last;
But e'en thy fading into day
　　　　Brought me an echo of the past.
'Twas this,—how fair my life began;
　　　　How pleasant was its hour of dawn;
But, merging into sorrow's day,
　　　　Then beauty faded with the morn."

from "Morning on Shinnecock," by Olivia Ward Bush-Banks
(1869–1944). First published in *Original Poems*
(Press of Louis A. Basinet, 1899).

No Quiero

Money is the most important thing in this world. My coworker at the children's museum said this wistfully, looking out at the mini-golf. *This* world, with all its unquestionable natural beauty, was just as expensive as the city, so I agreed. I freelanced, had this part-time job, and taught college while in graduate school, all so I could pay for gas to make it to these jobs.

The museum mothers dripped paint on canvases in tailormade studios in Sag Harbor cottages. Or spoke on the phone a great deal, about shipments and meetings and fabulous things. They smelled like Le Labo's Santal 33. They walked past us without checking in because they were members of the museum, maybe even esteemed donors, and we were supposed to know who they were. Sometimes they would actually say, *Do You Know Who I Am.* They walked past us to pick up their children. The nannies, Salvadoran or Mexican or Guatemalan or Colombian, handed them over. Sometimes the children cried at the sight of their mothers, maybe because they didn't recognize them for a second, maybe because they didn't want to go home. They almost always spoke perfect Spanish. *No quiero*, they'd say, blond and exquisitely dressed, pressed against a brown thigh.

Diet Coke

My mother retired from the hospital where she had worked for 30 years around the time Beba died. She was 50. She preferred to cash out than be forced to use email or the internet, even though those skills had been part of the job description for assistants since the mid-1990s.

Since then, she has found the right medication, but hasn't stopped drinking. She travels every three months, despite low funds, despite Covid, always in a group, always a planned tour. She still uses a travel agent. I am still her pelúa. She still calls almost every day. During a two-week episode in 2021, she cleared the hoard in my father's old office and my childhood bedroom. Sold some of it, put most of it out with the trash. I haven't been home since 2019. It becomes harder to return, the more apparent the distance I've put between my country and me becomes.

≈

The morning María hit PR, I was at a writing workshop titled "The Story You Are," where we all had to share what we thought our fellow writers' stories—meaning, the thing toward which they'd write for the rest of their lives—would be. These strangers said mine was "home." On graduation day two years later, my thesis advisor gave me *One Hundred Years of Solitude* in Spanish and English as a gift, even though I had never spoken about or felt particularly attached to Gabriel García Márquez's work. He told the white Hamptons audience about a tale of resilience—one he claimed was mine—that I didn't identify with. Things about my parents, my grandparents. I felt more like the people in the audience than my grandparents' granddaughter.

≈

A couple of weeks after María, my mother called me from her car. Before then, she had called me a handful of times for two minutes or less to update me on the state of things to preserve her battery. She said she had been waiting for gas for three hours. Her friend Angeles had driven up at the same time so they could roll down their windows and talk to each other in line. There was always a chance that the pump would be empty by the time they got to it, so they had to make the time count for something. *Lines*, she said, *my life is made up of lines now.* She was running out of pills, and prescriptions and claims weren't going through to the pharmacy. But she had found the only bar with a generator. *I had a few drinks because there wasn't Diet Coke. There's no Diet Coke left on the island, can you believe this*, she said, like it was the most disastrous thing. I asked her if she had eaten. She said, *Don't worry about me. You keep going.*

≈

I mailed her eight gallons of Diet Coke that day. They didn't make it in.

Flooding in San Juan's Calle Loíza after Hurricane María, September 21, 2017.

Meschutt Beach

One night a month later, in early October, I went for a swim at Meschutt Beach, close to the house I lived in. I stared up at the moon as I floated, as the place I was from crumbled and I started yet again. I was freezing and far away. Ashamed about feeling safe in that water, about having chosen to work with my hands the past summer when my ancestors didn't have a choice. About dropping everything and running whenever things were too much, about being alone, about taking nature for granted, as if it would be there when I got back from burning houses. But that night there was also a tenderness between my dead and me, an understanding that we all do what we can to hold still in the thrashing. I haven't stopped moving since.

Image Credits and Works Consulted

Page xv: Map of Puerto Rico from 1898 including Mona (on the southwest), Vieques, and Culebra (east of the big island). Map first appeared in *Puerto Rico and Its Resources*, by Frederick Albion Ober (D. Appleton and Company, 1898).

Page xviii: Trajectory of major land-falling cyclones (categories 3, 4, and 5) in Puerto Rico from 1928 to 2017. Map generated with NOAA's Historical Hurricane Tracks online tool. Retrieved on March 1, 2023.

Page 13: Plantation and sugar mill in Caguas circa 1900. From Strohmeyer & Wyman, Publisher. Plantation and sugar mill at Caguas,—between San Juan and Guayama,—Porto Rico. Puerto Rico, 1899. Photograph. https://www.loc.gov/item/2018663665/.

Page 17: de Burgos, Julia. Lines from "Río Grande de Loíza" from *Song of the Simple Truth: The Complete Poems of Julia de Burgos,* translated by Jack Agüeros. Willimantic: Curbstone Press, 1997. p. 9.

Page 31: Sterilization statistics taken from Ordover, N. (2014, February 24). Puerto Rico. Retrieved July 29, 2022, from https://eugenicsarchive.ca/discover/tree/530ba18176f0db569b00001b.

Page 43: Farms in the hills of Corozal circa 1941. Delano, Jack, photographer. Corozal, Puerto Rico vicinity. Small farms in the hill country. United States Puerto Rico Corozal Municipality Corozal, 1941. Dec. Photograph. https://www.loc.gov/item/2017797217/.

Page 73: Satellite image of Hurricane Georges making landfall on Puerto Rico on September 21, 1998. Image courtesy of the University of Wisconsin-Madison/Cooperative Institute for Meteorological Satellite Studies.

Page 84: Damage to homes in Toa Baja, Puerto Rico, on October 1, 1998, about a week after Hurricane Georges. FEMA photo by Dave Gatley (in the public domain). National Archives at College Park, College Park, MD [retrieved from the Access to Archival Databases at www.archives.gov, January 17, 2023].

Page 120: Official vs. estimated death tally after Hurricane María. Kishore, Nishant et. al. "Mortality in Puerto Rico after Hurricane María" *New England Journal of Medicine* 379, no. 2 (July 2018): 162–170. https://doi.org/10.1056/NEJMsa1803972.

Page 133: Bush-Banks, Olivia Ward. Lines from "Morning on Shinnecock" from *Original Poems*. Providence, RI: Press of Louis A. Basinet, 1899.

The following eight images (all in the public domain) are reprinted courtesy of the National Oceanic and Atmospheric Administration:

Page 1: Weather map of San Felipe Segundo nearing Puerto Rico on September 13, 1928.

Page 27: Weather map of Hurricane San Ciprián right over Puerto Rico on September 27, 1932.

Page 49: Satellite image of Hurricane Hugo over Puerto Rico on September 18, 1989.

Page 64: Damage in Culebra Island, Puerto Rico, on September 18, 1989.

Page 95: Satellite image of Hurricane Sandy over northeastern United States.

Page 106: An overflight shows some of the damage that Hurricane Sandy caused when it hit the New Jersey coast at the end of October 2012.

Page 113: Satellite image of Hurricane María over Puerto Rico, completely covering the island on September 20, 2017.

Page 137: Flooding in San Juan's Calle Loíza after Hurricane María, September 21, 2017.

Acknowledgments

Earlier versions of the following pieces have been published elsewhere:

"Pedro/Buelo," published as "Hurricane San Felipe II Made Grandpa an Agnostic." *Radar Poetry*. Issue 29. Feb. 2021

"The Man You Don't Understand Sings Himself to Sleep." *Salt Hill Journal*. Issue 43 (Print). Mar. 2020

"Old Wives' Tales." *The Brooklyn Rail*. June Issue (Print and Online). Jun. 2018

"Keepsakes." *The Southampton Review*. Summer/Fall 2018

I'm sincerely grateful to Kathleen Rooney and Abigail Beckel for taking a chance on this manuscript and shepherding it with thoughtful, meticulous care.

Writing is lonely, but I'm lucky to have these people around: Donald Breckenridge, who has been reading my drafts and writing recommendation letters for 15 years and counting, despite my changing jobs and personalities every few months; Marian Donahue, who has coffee with me every Sunday; Alana Mohamed, Julian Rostek, Miranda Beeson, Max Parker, Grace Dilger, and Jeremy Wang-Iverson. Thanks to my friends for their notes, for talking me off multiple ledges, for making me dinner, and for getting me gigs. Thanks to my mother for giving me permission to talk about things that we don't want to talk about.

I'm also grateful for the financial support of Stony Brook University, where I wrote the first draft of *The Hurricane Book* and met some of my favorite people; for the Flamboyán Foundation/Mellon Foundation; and for the countless jobs for which Donald Breckenridge wrote me recommendation letters. Thanks also to John Bateman at NOAA for his photo guidance, to Jason Alejandro for the cover, and to Valerie San Filippo for correcting my mistakes.

About the Author

Claudia Acevedo-Quiñones is a writer from Puerto Rico whose poems and short fiction have appeared in *The Brooklyn Rail*, *wildness*, *Ambit Magazine*, *Radar Poetry*, and other publications. In 2019, she received an MFA in Creative Writing and Literature from Stony Brook University, where she also taught poetry to undergraduate students. Her chapbook, *Bedroom Pop*, was published by dancing girl press in 2021. In 2022, she was awarded a Letras Boricuas Fellowship by the Flamboyán Arts Fund and the Mellon Foundation. Claudia lives in Brooklyn, New York.